Awakening
Body
Consciousness

For all those who,
through thousands of years,
have dedicated themselves to keeping
the inner life alive,
nourished it with their questioning,
sustained it with their love
and the sensitivity of their physical, mental and
emotional bodies—
through deserts of uncertainty
to the shores of the boundless sea.

Awakening Body Consciousness

Seven Steps to Integrating Body, Mind and Heart

PATTY DE LLOSA

sussex
ACADEMIC
PRESS
Brighton • Chicago • Toronto

2 4 6 8 10 9 7 5 3 1

First published in 2020 by
SUSSEX ACADEMIC PRESS
PO Box 139
Eastbourne BN24 9BP

Distributed in North America by
Independent Publishers Group
814 N. Franklin Street, Chicago, IL 60610

British Library Cataloguing in Publication Data
A CIP catalogue record for this book is available from the British Library.

Library of Congress Cataloging-in-Publication Data
To be applied for.

Paperback ISBN 978-1-78976-045-3

Typeset & designed by Sussex Academic Press, Brighton & Eastbourne.
Printed and bound by CPI Group (UK) Ltd, Croydon, CR0 4YY

Contents

CONTENTS

Acknowledgments

A lifetime of living, learning, and experiencing went into this book, and many influences have shaped it. First and foremost, I was brought up within the teaching of G. I. Gurdjieff by amazing parents who were part of the first generation of teachers of his ideas. I am most grateful to them for all they have shared with me. I also wish to acknowledge with gratitude and affection the many companions with whom I have studied the Gurdjieff ideas and sacred dances, always a guiding star.

My early studies also included Hindu and Buddhist texts as I sought to develop more consciousness. Then, when I was thirty, my mentor Jeanne de Salzmann, who guided the Gurdjieff teaching after his death, suggested I study Tai Chi. I turned to master T. T. Liang, just arrived from Formosa, became his student, and discovered the central importance of grounding. Recent work with Qigong masters Yang Yang and Robert Peng has continued to deepen my appreciation for that path to the development of Being.

After the break-up of my marriage I turned to C. J. Jung and other experts in psychology to understand better the unconscious forces that drive us. Work with Jungian analyst Marion Woodman and her *BodySoul Rhythms* intensives helped me find renewal in body and soul.

Later, when I retired as deputy chief of reporters of *Fortune* magazine, I took the three-year training to become an Alexander Technique teacher, which provided new insights into Body Consciousness. Also at that time, in an attempt to span the seemingly irresolvable divisions between science and the sacred, I began to delve into neuroscience.

Much thanks to Publisher Jeff Zaleski and the inspirational group of editors and writers who make *Parabola* so unique. Readers of that magazine will recognize some of the ideas expressed here, which I have touched on in my articles as contributing editor. Joyful gratitude to Pavi and Nipun Mehta and the amazing worldwide Service Space team I work with as a volunteer editor of *The Daily Good*. Finally and especially, a grateful salute to editor Anthony Grahame and his talented cohorts at Sussex Academic Press who have guided my last two books from manuscript to published copy.

"Sensation is the essential experience on the road to consciousness."

Jeanne de Salzmann

"Your mind is in every cell of your body."

Candace Pert

"Matter is spirit moving slowly enough to be seen."

Teilhard de Chardin

"If you have no experience of the wisdom of the conscious body, you are in unknown territory, listening to your mother tongue."

Marion Woodman

Introduction

Every time we focus on our ever-unfolding sensate experience we return to the present moment, because the kinesthetic sensation of the body-self is always here. It's like the river you can never step into twice because it continually changes. *Awakening Body Consciousness* presents many ways to connect mind with body and soul through intensifying the sensation of our *presentness* here and now.

When we turn the mind's attention toward the body, all it contains becomes more alive as well. Can you think of one aspect of the search for soul or spirit that doesn't begin from the body? In fact, without a body, where would spirit land? It is the nexus where soul and spirit connect with the actively thrumming life energy within us. And every time we bring body and mind into relationship with each other, Body Consciousness awakens.

Here's an example: my fingers are tapping these very words into the computer at the same moment that my brain formulates them. I could choose to be aware of my fingers and hands, and include the living fact that my butt is resting on the chair and my feet touching the ground. However, I'm often locked into a concentrated mindset as I write, with little or no sensation of how or where I am.

Whatever position you find yourself in right now, try tuning in to your Body Being. As your hands grasp a paperback or some electronic device to read these words, remind yourself that this book is talking to your hands as well as your head. Then open your awareness to include the living experience of all of you, *right here, right now.*

Awakening Body Consciousness integrates recent discoveries in neuroscience with millennial wisdom. Both affirm that our bodily presence is the bridge between the *I-consciousness* within all of us—and this *AM*, the Being that lives in the world. Therefore, whether your aim is spiritual development, to practice your own presence in the world, or just to live more richly—more centered in your essential Being—this book has been written for you. All you need is a wish to free yourself from habitual attitudes, and a will to explore new approaches to conscious action.

These seven steps to integrating body, mind, and heart are gathered from many decades of work with master teachers as well as my own personal experiences in a lifelong exploration of spiritual paths and ways of healing. Brought up in the teaching of G. I. Gurdjieff, I studied his ideas and learned the sacred dances and movements from him at an early age, then went on to teach them to others. After his death, Jeanne de Salzmann carried on his work and was my mentor. At age thirty I learned Tai Chi from master T.T. Liang, and have practiced and taught it ever since.

When I was in a depressed state following a broken marriage, I turned for help to the work of C. G. Jung and attended some of Jungian analyst Marion Woodman's BodySoul Rhythms intensives. Later I left my job as deputy chief of reporters at *Fortune Magazine* for the three-year training to become an Alexander teacher. I have led groups and individuals in the Gurdjieff Work, Tai Chi, Qigong and the Alexander Technique for many years, as well as engaged in extensive research in world religions, psychotherapy, and neuro-science—both for myself and as an editor of *Parabola* magazine and the *Daily Good*.

The fact is, thought alone cannot transform our life-on-earth into a meaningful experience. And without meaning, what is life? Body Consciousness is the necessary ingredient in the work toward the growth of Being. The body contains its own awareness and intu-ition, its sense of belonging to a Self, plus the functions we require in order to experience ourselves in action and repose. Our DNA, our psyche, the hands that create and the minds that invent—all are aspects of the living body, and dependent upon it.

In *The Reality of Being* Jeanne de Salzmann offers an appropriate prayer to open our investigation into Body Consciousness: "I wish to be conscious of this unknown energy that is in me. For this I need to get rid of the idea that I know my body. I must see that the memory of my body, of the known sensation of my body, imposes itself as an answer at the moment of questioning who I am, the moment of incomprehension. And because this answer appears spontaneously, I remain passive and do not wake up and look. I must see this constant tendency to let the memory of sensation preempt the direct perception. I need to see that my body is also unknown."

Like me, you have probably spent much of your life collecting aches and pains as well as emotional repercussions. But who is this Self, this somebody-who-has-been-here-all-the-time, and lives in another room of our inner mansion? My hope is that *Awakening Body Consciousness* will help you discover a deeper sense of your own presence during daily activities as you strive for a full-bodied awareness of Self and World. May light and fresh air stream in as you open to the greatness that lies within you.

STEP ONE
Activating Our Fundamental Power

Why Body Consciousness?
"Man is a citizen of three worlds, in which, even now,
he has his Being."
Sri Krishna Prem

After many years of trying, failing, and from time to time awakening to a finer energy in myself, I've concluded that my task on earth is to develop Body Consciousness. Here's why: This Body Being is the house I live in—the launching pad for every effort I make, from the highest quality of thought and heart intertwined, to habitual, mindless functioning when I move along on autopilot.

Our human dilemma lies in the fact that we contain three worlds that are seldom in sync with each other. Are we thinking animals? Are we minds dragging a body along behind us? And why is it so difficult to open the heart, the essential third element which has the power to unite the other two?

These three *centers of activity* are the transmitters and receivers of all our experiences of ourselves and the world. They are our instinctive, emotional, and mental hubs. Each has its own location in the body—in the belly, the chest, and the head. Our spinal column unites all three through the central nervous system.

While they could work together in harmony, they mostly operate as separate worlds within us. That means our life-energy can be caught like a butterfly in the net of the wandering or over-focused mind, dragged down into aches, illness and fatigue, or erupt in emotional reactions.

Each of us tends to act or respond most frequently from one of these three hubs. In one person, the body will almost always come first; in another, an emotional reactor experiences life; and in a third, the mind floats above it all.

How about you?

Imagine that you contain three bells, each of which sounds out its own note—low, middle and high. At any moment one of them can drown out the other two with its clamor. Unfortunately for us the bell ringer, who could form a harmonious chord with them, tends to be asleep at the job. That means any one of these three receiving and transmitting stations of our life's activity can absorb all our attention as we forfeit awareness of the other two.

How to bring body, mind, and heart into a balanced relationship with each other under a common authority—that of your essential Self? As you move through your day, notice which of them takes over at any moment. Discover how hard it is to slow down the flow of turning thoughts when your head usurps the throne of your inner castle, and that you have even less control over the reactions stirring in your chest. But—aha! When you focus consciously on the sensations of your Body Being, all those busy thoughts and emotional reactions tend to quiet down. Your attention begins to gather and your tensions recede.

As your consciousness expands, you may sense a finer energy in and around you, as if heaven has come down to fill your personal earth. You may also perceive a different quality of vital energy that enters you from below, because our small individual span of life is nourished from both directions. As soon as we become present to the flow of energy from both directions, Body Consciousness awakens.

Neuroscientists tell us we register impressions of the world and ourselves either through top-down or bottom-up information processing. Our thought-oriented efforts start with the big picture, and break it down into smaller parts. Each part is then refined several times to reduce it to the basic elements of which it is made.

But the intellect is not always our best guide. It often functions in an automatic flow of thoughts and associations—each bumping into the next without our conscious participation. Only when we intentionally focus our attention on a specific topic does this mental flow of mixed judgments, opinions, commentaries, and criticisms of ourselves (and everyone else) temporarily cease. At that point the automatic mechanism is replaced by a more conscious effort to solve a problem, make a decision, or simply become aware of what's happening right now.

Bottom-up processing starts with sensory experience and works toward integration in the mind. Neuroscientist Daniel Siegel calls it by the Zen term, Beginner's Mind. He explains that while the brain can change states very fast, the body is unable to keep up with it.

In *The Body Keeps the Score: Brain, Mind and Body in the Healing of Trauma,* psychiatrist Bessel van der Kolk insists that any hope of staying in control of your world depends on having a friendly relationship with your body. Without it, you grab for outside help "from medication, drugs like alcohol, constant reassurance, or compulsive compliance with the wishes of others." His many years of research with sufferers of PTSD have brought him to recognize the fundamental importance of bodywork in rehabilitation.

Regrettably, belief in the superiority of the head brain has dominated western thought for the last four hundred years, in spite of the fact that our intellectual, problem-solving energy will never be powerful enough to take us home in ourselves. While mental focus is fundamental to our search for understanding, there's a quality beyond intellect—a new level of *intelligence*—that includes both intellectual functioning and the deeper action of feeling.

Intellect can compare. Intelligence can choose wisely and with heart. And to activate that intelligence all we need to do is turn the great searchlight of the mind consciously on the enlivening experience of our Body Being. As we develop Body Consciousness—our fundamental power—we can work to prepare the ground (ourselves), so that mind, heart, and body can come together in a living moment of experience.

Are You Ready?
"Life is fired at us point blank."
Jose Ortega y Gasset

Sometimes we are visited by a moment of centeredness that's unforgettable. Perhaps in church or temple, perhaps in natural settings, or among those we love. That's when we begin to wonder whether another, more expansive inner life could be ours. Thousands of years of wisdom in prose and poetry confirm it. As Rainer Maria Rilke says in *I love my Being's dark hours,* "Then the knowledge comes to me that I have space within me for a second, timeless, larger life."

Aware of it or not, that second, larger life is what we seek, and perhaps it needs a second body to contain it, as postulated by many spiritual paths. In any case, the development of Body Consciousness, united with the heart's own sense of truth and the mind's best attention, offers a practical path for us to become truly present-in-the-world.

As Jungian analyst Marion Woodman explains in *Dancing in the Flames:* "'Body Consciousness' has an innate wisdom of its own . . . The more we realize the non-materiality of the body, of nature, the more conscious it becomes. This consciousness is what we call *soul,* a soul no longer forced into exile...This reanimation of the body allows us to enter consciously into the flow of life. We can dance in the flames, dying and being reborn in every moment, because the fear that cuts us off from life has been eliminated. The soul knows its immortality, and does not fear death as the ego does. Living from the point of consciousness allows us to live fully in the NOW."

One reason for our *exile* is the fact that physical intelligence eludes conscious thought. Scott Grafton points out in *Physical Intelligence: The Science of How the Body and the Mind Guide Each Other Through Life* that we are bemused by the mind's constant commentary. Because of it, we don't realize how much of the time our brain is actually engaged in "the raw physicality of being alive." The inevitable result: science views body and instinct as "a lower form of intelligence."

Yet the body is the vessel that contains all that is real and potential in us. Think of it as a musical instrument that can only play beautifully when all its strings vibrate in proper relationship to each other. That means we need tuning every day, perhaps every hour or every minute. And each time we re-enter the game of life with more of our Self, whatever has been held back becomes thankful to be called upon, to be in movement, to have a place in the world.

How to find the way to such readiness when we are bombarded all day long by life's demands on us? Pressured to respond to stimuli, whether in the mood or not, if we can bring our finest attention to each activity and risk, plunge, creep, or go headlong into body-conscious contact with life "without any possible postponement," as Ortega y Gasset recommends, we will meet its challenges with a ready instrument.

When Daniel Siegel affirms that "If we can change our thoughts we can change our brain," he means quite literally that we can work to change the 'hardware' in our heads. Any time you engage your body and your best thought at the same moment, the chokehold of habitual judgments and fixed attitudes as to how things ought to be will release.

Check in with your chest to see what you are feeling at this very moment. Probably your mind is hurrying your organism along. Ask yourself a few questions about your feelings out loud. Note that as you listen to your own voice, your thoughts slow down. However, soon the monkey mind will jump back in to explain everything, and you will no longer stand at the doorway of a discovery about yourself.

That's when a choice appears—do you want to be quicker or more aware? A longing to be present awakens even as your mind urgently wants to press forward to answer any doubts or fix any 'problems' as soon as possible. You are torn between the pull of habit on the one hand, and the possibility of a new global awareness on the other. This is a moment Jungians call *living in the tension between the opposites*. It is the portal to a new experience of yourself.

Stay with the sensation of your Body Being in the midst of this uncomfortable tug-of-war between your wish and your habitual thought-forms. Then, as you deepen the experience of Body Consciousness, you will find that it is possible to be sensitive and alert rather than mesmerized by whatever you are thinking, feeling, or doing. The work you are engaged in will move right along without the physical tension, without the emotional stress.

Surprisingly, as you release your one-sided focus, "all things are added unto you." This experience awaits anyone who can sacrifice the state of urgency to allow native intelligence deep in our body/mind to step forward. But first we need to give up our old formulas and fixed ideas about how things *ought* to be done.

Adopting a New Attitude
"We don't see the world as it is. We see it as we are."
Anais Nin

Let's take an honest look at how we view what happens to us day by day. There's a major focus in the Western world toward comfort and the acquisition of money and worldly goods. But many less privileged countries have a different attitude toward life—even in situations where the future seems difficult, dangerous, or hopeless. In them your status as a human being traditionally comes first.

For example, in Muslim countries, instead of being greeted by "What are you up to these days?" or "How's it going with your to-do list?" you may be asked, "How is your *haal*?" When someone inquires about your *haal*, they are they are literally asking, "How is your heart doing right now, as you take this very breath?" They want to know whether you are feeling happy or sad, or any of a wide range of emotions.

From Africa comes the Zulu greeting *sawubona*, which means "I see you"—I see and respect your essential Being. And in India you will be greeted by *namaste*, which translates into "I salute the God in you"—the part of you that connects with the divine.

While you may feel imprisoned in your life situation with little hope of modifying it, the one thing you can always do is *adjust* your attitude. G. I. Gurdjieff suggests that you "cross to the other side of the street" inside yourself in order to think in a new way—actively shifting away from negative thoughts, criticism of others, yourself, and the conditions you live in.

Remember the Daoist story in which the farmer loses his most valuable possession, his horse? What a loss! Yet when it returns, bringing six other wild horses with it, what joy! But, oops, his son breaks his leg while taming one of them. Yet—what a relief—the boy is spared conscription into the army because of it.

Daoists believe that what seems bad leads to good, leads to bad, leads to good, and so on. The wise farmer in the story neither celebrates nor complains about each of these events, but stays alert to what will happen next. With such an attitude we take responsibility for whatever situation we are in—a wise alternative to accusing others or blaming life. In fact, according to Gurdjieff, wherever we are in life is the best possible place from which to begin work toward more conscious living.

"Not so easy," you might be muttering, and you are right. However, here's a master key to enjoying your life more: give up some of your expectations. Let go of all those *oughts* and *shoulds*. Ask yourself what you value most and spend more time on that, whatever form it takes.

It's never easy to give up our judgmental nature, our demandingness, our wish to have things *my way* above all else, but clarify for yourself who is so insistent within. You got it! The ego. Our little guy with a huge appetite for attention never factors in the price to the soul—an enormous cost in terms of the human need to find meaning in our lives.

Here's another useful practice: stop the flow of whatever you are engaged in from time to time to notice whether you are cruising along on autopilot. Who, at this moment, is present to your life? Gurdjieff suggests we invent alarm clocks to wake ourselves up from our habitual attitudes and ways of doing things.

Why not stop several times in your day today, over coffee, while washing your hands, even at your desk or in mid-movement, and close your eyes for a moment to see what's going on inside. What will you discover? A litany of complaints? Resentment or pleasure at whatever's happening at that moment? A general feeling-tone of anxiety? Or might you hear your own heart beating and your own soul calling you home.

As you become more aware of how the ego overwhelms your intentions, you can begin to lay down a new foundation from the ground up. Current studies in neuroplasticity show that by working to change our attitudes we can actually change the brain. We can replace our fixed ideas with a more positive mindset as we move to transform our lives.

Changing the Way the Brain Works
"The brain is neither immutable nor static, but continuously remodeled by the lives we lead."
Richard J. Davidson

Jeffrey Schwartz, a practicing neuro-psychiatrist affiliated with UCLA, and author of *Brainlock*, works with obsessive-compulsive disorder by teaching people how to change their thinking through a specific four-step program. A brief summary points up how useful it could be to all of us. Why not experiment with one of his steps each week for the next month.

His first step is to **Relabel** your negative thoughts, feelings, or behaviors. Here's an example: When I finally realized that the voice I'd always assumed to be my conscience was in fact a tyrannical inner judge who had no interest in my well-being, I began to call this hypercritical aspect of my personality by a new name. You can read more about it in my book, *Taming Your Inner Tyrant: A path to healing through dialogues with oneself.*

Once you recognize consciously the true nature of these inner voices by giving them a new name, you begin to separate yourself from them. They are not you! As Jung himself explains in *Memories, Dreams, Reflections*, "The essential thing is to differentiate oneself from these unconscious contents by personifying them, and at the same time to bring them into relationship with consciousness. (That is) the technique for stripping them of their power."

The second step would be to **Reattribute** those deep inner insistences. Recognize them for what they really are—*compulsions.* They are much stronger than your ordinary habits, and live on your energy. Frankly, they can eat you alive. As you consciously link their intensity to a biochemical imbalance in the brain that generates this pressure on you, you begin to develop a new attitude toward them.

Dr. Schwartz' third step is to **Refocus.** As soon as you recognize a compulsive habit, replace it immediately with a new and pleasant action—whether physical exercise, gardening, reading, writing poetry, painting, journaling, etc. He explains why that works: "The automatic transmission isn't working, so you manually override it. With positive, desirable alternatives—they can be anything you enjoy and can do consistently each and every time—you are actually repairing the gearbox.

"The more you do it, the smoother the shifting becomes. Like most other things, the more you practice, the more easy and natural it becomes, because your brain is beginning to function more efficiently, calling up the new pattern without thinking about it." In other words, if you can stick at it, your brain chemistry will create new patterns of behavior.

The fourth and final step is to **Revalue.** As you realize the old patterns never really worked for you and that another way of living is possible, even desirable, the intensity of your need for them will diminish. Remind yourself often that you are becoming a happier and healthier human being as you practice changing the chemistry of your brain.

Acknowledge that it will be quite difficult at first. It's as if all the old habits stood up and said, "No! This is *me*. Leave me alone!" But tell yourself out loud that it's *not* you. Then prove it to yourself. Here are a few experiments I have found especially useful: Notice which of the demands that come at you in your day you jump to respond to, and which you hold back from. Maybe you are like me, good at making to-do lists, but more involved in checking off items than in prioritizing them.

When you are overwhelmed by your list, ask yourself a pair of questions that might bring more balance to the moment: "What do I *need* to do right now?" "What do I *want* to do right now?" This is a good use of your inner critic. Then, based on a conscious reevaluation of which obligations are more important, postpone a fourth of your list to the following day.

As for your cell, let it ring. While the telephone is our ever-present means of communication with the world, we don't have to be slaves to it. Maybe you need to answer because of your job, but you can override the automaton who wants to grab it at the first ring. Let it ring three times as you allow the sound to penetrate (and perhaps irritate) your newly arising Body Consciousness. *Then* pick it up and respond. Another time, wait for two rings, or four—do anything that helps you stay alive to where you are in time and space.

Dissolving the Habits that Imprison Us
"How have you used yourself today?"
F. M. Alexander

In a recent Harvard study by Matthew Killingsworth and Daniel Gilbert, more than two thousand people were called in the middle of their workday and asked what they were thinking about. It turns out that forty-seven percent of the time their minds were not focused on what they were doing.

Even more striking was the fact that they felt less happy when their minds were wandering. Those who learn how to focus their attention on the present moment are good athletes, good listeners, good thinkers, and good workers at anything they do, because this gathering of the attention moves mind, heart and body toward a more balanced state of awareness, of readiness to act.

While we may be distracted a lot of the time, the minute we seriously ask the question, "Where am I?" we are right here and now. Problem is, as soon as we stop asking, we're back in our habitual ways of thinking and acting. What can help free you from the habits that interfere with being present to your life?

Doing something new each day is a good way to begin. Consciously plan something you seldom or never try. That will stir the prefrontal cortex into action. Intentionally open a conversation with someone you avoid. You may discover a new basis for communication. You might even make a friend. Taste a food you've never eaten. Go to work by a different route each day. Whether walking to the subway, driving to the office or taking time for a brisk walk, forge a new path.

The same wake-me-up call is available in your home. Invite yourself to put on the other shoe first for a week, then change back. Challenge yourself to use your other hand as your pour your coffee or brush your teeth. The *uber* neuro-improvement challenge will be to learn to write with your other hand. Becoming ambidextrous is a royal road to refreshing the brain, like learning a new language.

The most difficult of all habits to change is that of hurrying. What a shame that modern life has pressed us to the point where it has become a compulsion. But here's another opportunity to shift the way your brain works. Hurrying speeds you away from the present moment, expressing a wish to be in the future because maybe you'll be late. To counter it, master Alexander teacher Walter Carrington tells his students to repeat each time they begin an action: *"I have time."*

We are bombarded all day long by stimuli that call us to immediate action, but the pause of saying *"I have time"* summons an alternative mode in the nervous system. It inhibits the temptation to rush forward under the automatic mandate, "do it now!" Try this sometime when you're in a hurry—send yourself a message to delay action for a nano-second before you jump into the next activity. Even say it out loud to yourself.

When you hold back your first impulse to go into movement by creating a critical pause during which your attention is gathered, you become present to the moment you are living through. At that point you can choose to respond rather than react. Even in the middle of myriad demands, telling yourself *"I have time"* can provide a mini-break to the nervous system—a moment of choice.

Then you can remind yourself to attend to your Body Being as you press forward with your work. Why not release the tensions gathered at the back of your neck, shoulders, and lower back before you commit to the next task? You have *every right* to interrupt whatever you are doing to stretch out of the fixed position you are in and into the present moment.

You may well ask, "How can I be expected to stay in the present moment when I need to finish this job?" When you *have* to get something done in a hurry and there's no time to lose, try these five steps. First, acknowledge how you really feel about the job. Hate it or love it, let your reactions appear in your conscious awareness. Accept them, whatever they may be. "That's how it is at this moment."

Second, turn to the only remaining place where freedom is available: within yourself. Notice the thoughts that are a-thinking in you and turn them to focus on the job in front of you. Third, bring your attention to the moves your hands are making. Acknowledge their superior intelligence, the many things they know how to do without your thinking about it. Sense the tapping of your fingers on computer, ipad, or cellphone; revel in the warm soapy water you are washing in; or feel how the strong arm and back muscles engage as you lift something heavy or press a freshly glued object together.

Fourth, begin to explore other parts of your body, starting with the back of your neck, where stress tightens your muscles into tough guy ropes that pull the head forward and down out of alignment. Let your thought move wherever the body moves, seeking out the tense corners and inviting release.

Fifth, if you are sitting, interrupt whatever you are doing from time to time, no matter how important, to get up or at least stretch out and away from the position you are in. Since everything is connected in the mind/body continuum, you might be surprised to what extent you can relieve your stressed-out system with a brief, non-essential walk down the hall, a peek out the window at the larger world, or even a seriously deep sigh that engages you right down to the toes.

Do *anything* to interrupt the deadening bond that glues all your attention to what you're writing, reading, cooking, chopping, building. Truly, the body possesses wisdom that thought doesn't understand. We can practice listening to it and allow ourselves to expand into Body Consciousness. *"I have time"* helps us do just that.

Neutralizing Judgmental Attacks

"We not only need to know more about ourselves, we also need to love more of ourselves."
Thomas Moore

One reason undertaking a new program is so difficult is that we get annoyed with ourselves when we don't immediately succeed at making the changes we seek. Tune in to the dissonance that exists between your three parts. Does it seem as if head and heart move along the road to spiritual development hauling your body behind them? It may sometimes feel that way.

Yet when the body comes alive, everything it contains comes alive as well. Any intentional effort to move away from the status quo nourishes the spirit. So take a step back when your inner world becomes a war zone of self-recrimination. Neuroscientists track how brain and body respond instantly to our emotional habits. They tell us we short-circuit our own well-being each time we accuse ourselves of "there-I-go-again."

This can run the gamut from accidentally breaking a cup, to saying something hurtful or offensive to a friend, or much worse. You've probably heard the expression, "what fires together wires together." It means that every experience, every thought, every feeling, and every physical sensation, triggers thousands of neurons to form a neural network. It is the repetition of such mental states that leads to our habitual attitudes.

Here's how our ongoing habit of criticizing ourselves works against us, courtesy of Wendy Suzuki, professor of neural science and psychology at New York University: "If I remember an incident in which I failed in some way and immediately add the thought that I was stupid or inadequate—in other words, attack myself at the moment I remember the incident—I'm connecting two formerly unrelated mind events and their respective neuronal activity.

"What's bad about this is that I'm emphasizing or demonizing my failure out of proportion to its real effect and making that connection, that negative self-attack, part of the memory of the incident. But if I could bring a modicum of reasoning or self-forgiveness to it, acknowledging that I'm human, or forgot, or didn't know enough, or was unprepared to make the right decision, or whatever is appropriate, over time my new thinking will affect the neural structure of my brain, synapse by synapse.

"This is an example of the *neuroplasticity* scientists speak about so much these days—your brain has been forming and changing ever since before you were born and will continue to do so until you take your last breath."

If self-recrimination is your habit, tell yourself you are not *unsatisfactory*, you are *unfinished*. There's work to be done to become the real, unvarnished *you*, and you have been given a lifetime in which to do it.

One way to shift your attitude is the glass-half-full exercise. When you catch yourself making some accusation about yourself or someone else, quickly describe it in an alternative way. For example: I'm sitting at my desk, and as I reach for the phone I spill coffee on some papers I was proofing. Darn! How stupid was that! "But wait," my new attitude says to my old self, "thank the Lord I didn't spill it on my tablet!"

What's good about that? It clips off the flowering of self-attack and focuses my thought in a new direction—on the work I'm doing. The basic message to any neural network stuck in past habits: *Let it go and move on!*

Such an exercise may seem minor but, as Rick Hansen explains in *Buddha's Brain*: "Because of all the ways your brain changes its structure, your experience *matters* beyond its momentary, subjective impact. It makes enduring changes in the physical tissues of your brain, which affect your well-being, functioning, and relationships. Based on science, this is a fundamental reason for being kind to yourself, cultivating wholesome experiences, and taking them in."

Sitting by the Well
"Let silence take you to the core of life."
Rumi

Nevertheless, even the most dedicated among us will have dark days when nothing seems to go right. When that happens, and I don't know what to do next, I sit down by the Well of Being—just sit there, and listen to myself, and the world. The well is deep. I feel that in my bones. Perhaps it's bottomless.

When I'm in anguish or at wit's end, I've learned that nothing will change until I sit down by the well and give up all the explanations for what's wrong, as well as efforts that have brought me relief in the past. There's nothing more to do but sit and wait.

Acknowledging your ignorance is essential when you open to the unknown. Lost in a suddenly alien world, you may wonder, will help come? It usually does but don't assume it will, because then you are bargaining with the universe in order to get things to go your way.

Sit there, listening. Sit there with all you've got. Notice your thoughts upstairs as they pass by like clouds, and your bursts of reaction like sparks of energy in the chest: agreement, disagreement, discouragement; I like, I don't like; I want, I don't want. Then turn your focus on your body, sitting there in real time, legs sinking into the floor, butt perched on a chair, as your torso rises like a tree trunk and your head floats on top.

When I recently learned that a dear, dear friend has cancer, I sat by the well with my heart/mind shouting, "it cannot be so!" Anguish rose and swirled around my chest, impeding my breathing. Tears fell, but I scarcely paid attention to them. Finally the pain settled down into a dull ache, and gradually a larger energy surged up from below, from the bottomless well.

This Well of Being isn't ours, even though it is always available to us. It can connect us with a source of energy we seldom contact as the demands of life pull us along. Unfortunately, when we have refreshed ourselves from its depth, we pop right back up to the surface of ourselves as soon as we go into action.

Where is the bridge between those depths and our daily life? Marion Woodman alerts us in *Conscious Femininity* that, "If we have no bridge to the unconscious depths that drive us, our rational attempts to correct our situation are merely Band-Aids. They work only so long as we remain cut off from the living fire inside. When that fire blazes forth, our Band-Aids go up in smoke."

Body Consciousness is that bridge. To learn more about how to rekindle your fire and send those Band-Aids up in smoke, let's move on to the Second Step, ***Coming to Your Senses.***

STEP TWO
Coming to Your Senses

Listening to The Call from Below

"Body awareness puts us in touch with our inner world, the landscape of our organism."
Bessel van der Kolk

When the searchlight of the mind is turned on our vehicle, a deeper level of feeling arises. Nothing is more powerful in support of our awakening consciousness than connecting our thought with our body. Lucky for us that we have many senses to keep us hitched to our earthly selves and the flow of life: touch, taste, smell, hearing, seeing, and the kinesthetic awareness of where we are in space.

Body Consciousness plays a huge part in our relationships as well. The mind doesn't feel—it judges, chooses, and disposes of ideas, things, and even sometimes people. That is the basis for all kinds of discrimination, both creative and repugnant. Martin Buber's seminal *I and Thou* alerts us to the ever-present danger of treating others not as the vulnerable human beings we all are, but as an *it*. That's what the head does when neither feeling nor body is present to the encounter.

You can also apply Buber's 'I' and 'it' differentiation to your relationship with your own physicality. Your body is not an *it*, but a *thou*, a partially unknown being. As Marion Woodman makes clear in *Dancing in the Flames*, "Without our recognition of the sweetness and sadness, rage and hope, in our bodies, and our honoring of our limitations as human bodies, we have no way of experiencing our compassion for one another."

Therefore, when you feel lost and wish to recover your sense of self-in-the-world, start at the bottom. To become aware of your feet supporting you from below is the beginning of saying *I am here*. It is fundamental to a sense of presence as well as the foundation for all martial arts.

Other paths to your present reality include responding sensitively to whatever you touch, tasting thoughtfully each mouthful of food, truly perceiving what you are looking at, and actively listening to yourself and the world. Gurdjieff speaks of "the right rhythms of the senses," saying that when we are connected to our own basic rhythms we come closer to who we really are.

To remain awake to the sensation of yourself, moment by moment, is never easy. Thoughts and associations will sidetrack you all day long, as well as judgments about how well or badly you're doing. Nevertheless, you can count on life's ups and downs to awaken in you sooner or later the anguished Socratic cry, *Who am I?* There you are, suddenly face to face with the deep unknown that is you.

Another powerful centering question is *Where am I?* It creates a place from which to begin the search for presence. When I queried myself just now, "Where in my body is my sense of self?" I discovered it was somewhere between the chest and throat—paper-thin and about a foot high. There was no sensation of my back or limbs at all. However, as soon as I became aware of this, more of me began to join the search for Body Consciousness.

Try asking it of yourself at different times in the day. See if you can catch the immediate internal response without adjusting anything. You will probably discover that your sense of self is momentarily confined to a small part of you. If so, ascertain how high, how wide? Is it two-dimensional or three-dimensional? Once you locate the place that seems to correspond to your self-of-that-moment, open to the experience of the rest of you. Go from top to toe or toe to top, and gradually include more width and depth as your mind seeks to fully occupy the space you live in.

To expand your kinesthetic awareness, all you need is a little healthy curiosity about what's going on and why you get so lost in outer doings. Here is where you really live! Return again and again to the full experience of yourself as flesh, blood, bone and brain, wakening to the possibility of being right here, right now.

Connecting with Flesh and Bones

"You can even get your head, connected with spirit, through the door of the temple, but the body may not be ready to follow."
Sri Krishna Prem

The grim news for those who sit still most of the day comes from recent research published in the *Annals of Internal Medicine*. Even if you exercise regularly you are likelier to leave the planet ahead of those who get up and move around more often. The most active people in the study, who sat for less than 30 minutes at a time, had a fifty-five percent lower risk than those who sat longer.

That should encourage you to get up out of your chair and go into action more often. The conscious shift of your focus toward flesh and bones reawakens Body Consciousness. As you turn the warmth of your attention on your neuromuscular self, it will respond— either by releasing tension or by letting you know where you are holding on tight.

One way to come alive to your self-in-action is to pay attention to your hands as they busy themselves with whatever work you ask them to do. What is your right hand up to? Is the left hand relaxed or tense? Find moments to sense how your two hands relate to each other as they work in concert. Have you noticed that they some-times seem more expert on how to do things than you are? It's as if they had a mind of their own and maybe they do. D. T. Suzuki, author of many books on Zen, famously said, "A man learns to think with his hands."

And how about your feet? Each is made up of twenty-six small bones. You can bet they would love to get out of your shoes and stretch themselves! At the end of your day, why not take each foot in your hands to explore its curves, joints, and boney places as you rub some sweet-smelling ointment on them. Say 'thank you' for their continuing service all these many years—a very small segment of you doing a very big job.

Whenever you stand up, find out right away where your weight is poised on them—front or back or sides? Do you tend to stand mostly on one leg? Remind yourself to stand equally balanced on both legs just to interrupt your habitual unconscious stance for a moment. Think about the meaning behind the expression, *standing on your own two feet*. Surely that is where you want to be!

Any time you sit—talking, texting, thinking—do you forget that your mind and hands have legs and feet under them? What are they into as you stare at the screen? Do they even exist for you at such a moment? Refresh yourself by acknowledging the biggest bone in your body, the femur, which is taking some of your weight right now. Its marrow works night and day to create new blood cells for you.

Now salute the knees, which bend at your beck and call. Then, say hello to your engineering marvel of a spine—the central pillar that holds you upright yet allows you to bend and twist. It is both thick and thin, made in segments so it can support the head and neck, anchor the ribcage, bear the weight and offer stability to your upper structure, as well as protect the spinal cord.

Those bones are twice as tough as granite so they can withstand the forces of compression, four times more resilient than concrete against stretching, and about five times as light as steel.

A lot is happening in the front of the torso where the heart beats as the liver processes, and other parts of a very busy digestive system work unceasingly to keep you going. Heart and breath are two great rhythms that dominate and support your Being and your health.

While you have little influence over the heartbeat, which tracks your emotional life, you have the possibility of a more conscious relationship with the diaphragm—the large, dome-shaped sheet of muscle that separates the chest from the abdomen. It plunges down and rises up to fill and empty the oxygen storage tanks of your lungs.

Finally, as you walk wherever you need to go, you could visualize your boney structure, the living skeleton that moseys along inside you—always there, holding you up, even though you are unaware of it.

Life energy—call it chi, ki, prana, pneuma, or elan vital—flows in and out with each breath. Simply by following the rhythm of your breathing without trying to change anything, you can connect more intimately with who you really are. Moment by moment the body responds to its inflow and outgo, as the mind becomes quiet and deeper feeling awakens. (More on breathing in Step Five).

Embodying the Soul

"What is the body? The body is merely the visibility of the soul, the psyche, and the soul is the psychological experience of the body. It is really one and the same thing."
C.G. Jung

Anchoring oneself in the body has always been central to mindfulness and meditation practices. More than a practice, it is a path. As Jeanne de Salzmann points out, "Our inner and outer posture is at the same time our aim and our way."

By seeking a conscious sensation of your grounded physical self and an awareness of the rise and fall of chest and belly with the breath, you come into direct contact with the energies coursing through you. Equally, in sitting meditation, a more complete awareness will flood in as you turn away from the thoughts that are a-thinking in you, and focus on listening to the larger life within your Body Being.

When the body is alive and open, a sense of clarity and intention fills us. Then along comes an emotion—a worry, a pressure, the memory of a personal slight—and the receptive field breaks up. The door to presence has slammed shut. What got in the way? Usually it's the onslaught of stimuli coming at us from all sides, along with our habitual responses to them.

Gurdjieff compares our habitual emotional reactions to a horse, pointing out that while you may be full of good intentions to do this or avoid that, "when the horse kicks" you are carried away. The Talmud informs us that a habit first enters as a guest, then becomes a family member, and finally takes charge. And Yoga master Patanjali invites us to see our bad habits as "tendencies" which can be circumvented by bringing conscious awareness to them.

Yet even when you discover that you are caught in a habitual state of unnecessary tension, help is right there where you are. Just bring your attention to your physical position—the mirror of your inner attitude. Any narrowed world-view will move away from habitual drives, reactions and tensions when you expand into a larger world that includes body, mind, and feeling.

To discover how your physical posture rules your emotional attitudes, try going into a deep slump for a couple of minutes. Then attempt to feel light and happy. Or sit up straight and look around you at whatever's happening nearby as you try to feel depressed. Notice whether, when you feel up-and-going, your body is leaning forward with an urgency to get something done fast. You may need to settle down a bit into legs and feet to get the job done well.

Are you drowning in your thoughts, with a slumped head and spine, furrowed brow, tensed jaw? Stand up straight and stamp hard a few times on the floor to activate your spinal juices and your sense of Self.

When you feel lethargic, the body's heaviness will often shift if you go into movement. A walk down the street might invigorate you. Or perhaps a telephone call to a friend would warm the heart and open that inner door to *presencing* yourself and the world around you.

All of our senses are gateways to Body Consciousness. For example, you can practice awareness of touch at any time. With each conscious contact a new message is given and received. Remind yourself often that *anything you touch touches you back*. Try to be more aware of what you touch today. Notice how picking something up offers an exchange of information—size, weight, maybe smell and sound as well. A piece of paper, a cell phone, a book, all carry sensory messages.

Human contact offers a deeper exchange of energy. We give and receive each other's vibrations all day long—sometimes intentionally, sometimes not. Touching or being touched by another living being helps you sense where and how you are. A touch can burn like fire, soothe like ointment, or fill the being with love. A firm handshake, a comforting hug, the softness of a baby's skin, or a loving sexual encounter will open you to a new awareness of the world and yourself.

As for taste, the food we eat nourishes soul as well as body. Sweet or sour, spicy or bitter, what we put into our mouths feeds us in many ways. While we often stoke ourselves mechanically when we eat while reading, watching TV, working at a desk, or talking, if we took more time to savor what we ingest we would be gifted with precious new impressions. What's more, to eat less and chew more provides a subtler enjoyment. And didn't Miss T. say that we *are* what we eat?

Smell is connected to taste and, like it, helps us select what's good for us and alerts us about what to avoid. Just for the pleasure of it, turn away from your busyness from time to time to take in any one of a cornucopia of perfumed scents and natural essences available to stir the body/mind toward action or repose. Investigate the Bach Essences, for example.

The fact is that the mind's attention, pulled in all directions by what's going on in and around us, is always in need of an anchor. When it is grounded in sensation, whether in a moment of deep stillness or vibrant action, a new level of feeling arises. Then, depending on how roundly we can listen to the singing in all our cells, Body Consciousness floods in, along with a sense of the sacredness of such a moment. At that point, the mind becomes a mirror and the body a temple.

Seeing Through the Eyes of a Tiger
"It is better to live for one day as a tiger than to live for a thousand years as a sheep."
Chinese proverb

Seeing is primarily receptive. We are witnesses to the world in spite of the fact that we are seldom able to take it all in. An intentional effort at perception allows us to receive and process impressions at a deeper level. As Gurdjieff reminds us, impressions are the most basic food for Being. We can live up to three weeks without ordinary food, little more than a week without water, around three minutes without air, but death is almost instantaneous in the absence of any impressions.

The eye is an amazing organ that works like the shutter of a camera—iris and pupil control the amount of light that gets in, while the lens helps you focus. Light rays are sent back to the retina, which receives them upside down and converts them to electro-chemical impulses. Then the optic nerve sends visual messages from retina to brain along a million nerve fibers.

It's the brain that controls what you see, combining images and turning them right side up again. What's more, because the visual cortex sits at the back of the head, you are actually looking out from the back of the brain.

Once you realize how far back your seeing takes place, you will no longer need to tense your eyeballs in an unconscious effort to grab what's in front of you and bring it back—an instinctive attempt to "take it all in." Instead, soften your gaze into receptivity, and let the world come to you as you look out from the back of the brain. Each time you remember to do that, your nervous system will shift into relaxation mode.

Here's a qigong exercise that invites you to "look through the eyes of a tiger." (In China the tiger is king of beasts). Stand firmly on both feet, shoulder width apart. Bend your knees gently and lean slightly forward from the hips as you make a triangle with your hands. Your two thumbs are at the bottom and first fingers almost touch each other above, palms facing out, about a foot in front of your face. As you look through the space within the triangle, breathe in and concentrate all your attention on a fixed point in front of you.

Then, as you breathe out, straighten up, arch slightly back, swing your elbows to the sides, forearms pointing upward, hands in fists, as you shift your gaze to panoramic awareness. Absorb everything in the room at once—all the people, things, colors, and movement around you. With your next in-breath, return to the first position and switch back to one-pointed focus. You can make this shift eight times for optimal results.

In this exercise you are learning to shift between two modes of vision: a focused, one-pointed concentration, and a panoramic awareness in which nothing goes unregistered by a relaxed gaze and a watchful mind. Both modes are necessary for survival in life as well as in the jungle. This practice also helps develop the deeper inner vision that is needed to shift back and forth from concentrating on one aspect of a decision to weighing all the alternatives within a larger perspective.

Ensouling the Body

"By inspiriting the body, the Spirit turns the body into a living body—an ensouled body. At the same time, by embodying the Spirit, the body helps ground the Spirit in time and space, making it real. Spirit and matter appear to seek each other through the psyche, and the place where they meet is the human soul."
Donald Kalsched

Neuroscientist Candace Pert points out in *Molecules of Emotion: The Science Behind Mind-Body Medicine* that "physicians treat the body with no regard for the mind or the emotions. But the body and mind are not separate, and we cannot treat one without the other." And since all emotions are expressed through the body, you will never have a clear idea what you are *feeling* except through bodily *sensations*.

How often do you express your feelings with such phrases as "I'm all choked up;" "he makes me sick;" "this is backbreaking work;" or "that makes my skin crawl"? As you explore the emotions that lie behind your inner aches and pains you will uncover clues to how to you *really* feel. You will learn at a deeper level whatever you need to know in order to relieve physical or emotional distress.

What is your habitual attitude to your physical self? For example, when you are all tuckered out, do you attack or embrace your Body Being? Take time to find out which brings you back into balance more quickly—cracking the whip or seeking a conscious connection with your energy in movement.

You may discover that when you turn your mind's best attention on your tired or discouraged body, you feel relief. Perhaps there will even be a suffusion of warmth, like the pleasure of recognition when you meet a friend. The body is always thankful when you include her in your awareness.

Or, on the other hand, you could investigate how many of your irritable or impatient moods are body-initiated: Are you using up all your energy pushing ahead with what your mind wants to get done? Could the body maybe just want a little time out, a few deep breaths, before going on to the next effort?

Marion Woodman reminds us in *The Ravaged Bridegroom* that, "As consciousness develops, the body will act as donkey for only so long. Men as much as women need to know that their soul is grounded in their own loving matter. 'This is who I am. Every cell in my body tells me this is of value to me—not to my persona, to me.' That is the container whose feeling can be trusted because it is grounded in reality."

When we listen more attentively to ourselves and the world, we reaffirm our own existence. Yet it is a huge challenge to stay rooted in one's own presence when speaking or listening to another person. How accurately do you process what others say? Can you take in what's behind the words you hear? Or are you sometimes too busy formulating a reply?

If so, go deeper. Tune in to your own body language next time you listen or speak to someone else. Notice whether you unconsciously narrow and compress your body in an attempt to "grasp" the other person's words. Or whether you lean forward when you are interested and shrink back when you feel aversion.

When you speak, your voice both expresses and influences the state of your Body Being. If you are consciously aware of the sounds you make, you will experience the vitality of your own vibrations. Share them with the world in clarification, friendship, story, or song. Speak from the heart to link parts of yourself that aren't always in contact with each other.

Sing often. Whether you intone noble themes in church, battle cries in action, anguished love songs in the dark of the night, or joyous arpeggios in the shower, singing awakens a part of you that gives deeper expression to what you feel.

Your vocal tone also tells you more about how and who you are. As you deepen your practice of Body Consciousness through speaking and listening, you will come into contact more often with your essential presence. Jeanne de Salzmann points out that "The role of our Presence is in connecting the two worlds . . . in fact, (it is) a spiritualization in which the spirit penetrates matter and transforms it."

Processing Pain as Information
"Your pain is the breaking of the shell that encloses your understanding."
Kahlil Gibran

When I'm hurt or become ill, I seek explanations and go for tests. Then the doctor tells me what's going on, and what to do about it. While my head takes it all in, I'm upset in my *feelings*. My plans are ruined. "Why me?" is a natural lament. It is also a question worth asking if we phrase it differently: "What is my body telling me aside from the fact that something's wrong?" I am invited to engage in *listening to the body.*

A familiar reminder. Yet we are often far from understanding what our bodily powerhouse of energies is telling us. A crash course in body listening could begin with learning about the physiology involved in whatever is off-kilter.

This becomes increasingly complex as physics and microbiology alter our view of the living body. Who knew there were more microorganisms in our gut than stars in the sky! And try to get your head around thirty-seven trillion cells in your body undergoing thousands of biochemical reactions every minute. The fact is, we are very sophisticated instruments.

While physical pain is unavoidable and doctors and drugs treat it as best they can, we need to learn how to process the emotional pain that resonates through us—to recognize and accept our emotions—feel what we feel.

Yoga, tai chi and mindful meditation can help ease chronic aches and pains. So can paying more attention to what our emotions are saying. But when we are focused on the next problem in the day's agenda, there's little time for the heart to speak. Or when the sense of loss seems too much to bear, our capacity to feel and sense may be held hostage in a general vise of tension—a refusal to take it all in.

In spite of the huge gulf between mind and body at such a moment, there is a shortcut. Bring your attention directly to the sensations that accompany your emotional state. Ask questions of your organism, like "What are you trying to tell me?" or "What is the one thing necessary for me to do right now?" And wait for guidance of an unaccustomed sort.

Such exchanges offer a new place from which to accept whatever we tried to avoid. Then, while we may not get rid of the body's ache or the heart's pain, life no longer runs away with us. We come face to face with our own living truth. And to work this magic we have only to begin an honest examination of what's really going on, in spite of the fact that it may hurt to do so.

Here's a minor example. As I walked to the subway one morning my whole body ached, rebelling at going to work. Shaken, I stopped short in the street and asked myself, "*Where* is this coming from?" Immediately my stomach responded with nausea, while at the same time the rest of my body relaxed and became free of pain. I walked on, wondering what had made me sick. Could it have been dinner the night before? Or something going on at office or home that I just couldn't stomach?

It's never easy in the midst of an active day to build a bridge to what's happening in the heart. Only with an effort of conscious attention to both physical pain and emotional constriction can you discover what's going on under your radar. Yet the body always offers immediate feedback—tense fingers, clenched jaw, stiffened legs, roiling stomach, or aching back. And if you are able to acknowledge rather than deny that something's wrong, your state will begin to change.

The difficulty lies in turning toward the pain rather than away from it. How to give up avoiding or refusing to face whatever cloud you are under till you 'feel better?' Try to open to whatever sensations and feelings appear without holding back. Accept that there's a hurt, reactive, complaining, fearful, angry, or just-plain-tired person within, who may have been there for a while.

No use arguing with pain, as in saying "I ought not to feel this way." The body is very honest. And your feeling reactions are real whether you want to feel them or not. Any avoidance thoughts like, "it's too late," or "there's no point worrying about it now," or simply, "I've got to grit my teeth and bear it" don't help. And while you don't have to grit your teeth, bearing the pain with awareness may be exactly what's required. That would allow its message to pass through you so you can move on.

Only when we accept to feel what we feel can we stand at the helm of our own ship, come about when we need to, and drop anchor. Then we can comply with the inner winds, the power of emotional tides, and learn whether the stars are in line with the course we set earlier. At that moment we become receivers of important information. As we listen to our own deeper nature by bowing to another presence that lives within us, we can begin to process whatever our pain needs us to know.

Collaborating with the Healer Within
Healing is a matter of time, but it is sometimes also a matter of opportunity.
Hippocrates

The first step in collaborating with illness is conscious recognition that I am in difficulty. That may sound simplistic, but some of us allow the demands of life and the desires of the mind to drive us on without much thought to what that pressure does to the body over time. That is, until something hurts. Or I'm suddenly short of breath. Or even in extreme cases, I have a stroke or heart attack.

The second step would be to apply our best thought to what's going on, even after the first diagnosis and treatment seems to cover all the bases. What we endlessly forget is that the body isn't made up of a lot of different, separate pieces, some of which may need to be 'corrected.'

When something hurts or gives out, we tend to formulate the problem in misleading terms like, "I've got a bad hip," or "I suffer from high blood pressure." As if the hipbone weren't connected to the thighbone, or high blood pressure was unrelated to what's going on in my life.

The fact is, we are organic moving entities who look at ourselves in a static way—engineering miracles whose whole structure can be pulled out of line when we lose contact with it. Pain and breathlessness call attention to a system-wide emergent difficulty. When my hip hurts it is because of something going on in the whole of my Body Being. The source may be an uneven pelvis, a slumped back, or the way I habitually drop my head forward or stick my chin out.

As for blood pressure, it may be high because a family member is out of line, in trouble, or because my boss always shouts and never recognizes the good job I've done. Or I didn't get what I wanted or thought was my due.

According to osteopathic physician and energy healer Steven Weiss, one of the major dilemmas in treating people with pain, especially chronic pain, is that the source of the problem is almost never where it hurts. Pain or symptoms need to be evaluated in terms of the whole body, how it is put together, and what it requires to heal.

"Doctors and therapists have the opportunity to transform themselves from practitioners who do things *to* the body, into informed listeners who work in cooperation *with* the body," he affirms. "Listening deeper, perceiving more, being more present, and striving to identify and heal problems at their source unlocks the infinite power of the body to heal itself."

Dr. Carolyn Dean, author of *The Magnesium Miracle,* who bridges allopathic and naturopathic medicine, points out that "The body doesn't get well by making damaged cells work correctly. It gets well by making new cells that work correctly. Every hour your body is creating 80,000,000 new cells! The body has the ability to heal itself of many ailments if it is supplied with sound nutrition and proper cellular energy."

And James Oschman, widely recognized as an authority on the biophysics of energy medicine, clarifies how the body and brain are connected. He points out that 'brain waves' are not confined to the brain, but actually spread throughout the body via the perineural system and the circulatory system. In other words, the entire nervous system acts as an 'antenna' that projects the *biomag-netic pulsations* that begin in the brain.

When we are hurt or sick, our instinctive Being focuses all its ener-gies on healing. However, the *doer* in us wants to move on in spite of the distress we feel. This runs counter to the healing process. So does the unconscious conviction that we need to hold onto ourselves so we won't fall apart. We are often caught between trying to ignore pain on the one hand or passively giving in to afflic-tion on the other.

So how to cooperate with the healer within? When you have no choice but to function fully while healing, tune in often to your body's needs and wishes. Embrace her as you go about your work with a consciously measured pace. Allow a little attention and sympathy for the wounded part. Above all, be cautious about what you sign up for in one 24-hour period.

When you finish one job ask your body, as if it were an intimate friend, whether it's all right to move on to what you thought to do next. Maybe it's time for a short break. Would a healing ointment, a soothing touch, a cookie or a drink of water help you get on with your work? Promise yourself some special treat when you finish. That way, you bring a feeling of choice to the effort.

Rituals can be useful in pressured situations when you are ill or in pain. Light a candle as you begin to work. The flame that accom-panies you represents the body/soul's needs. A moment of offering a prayer or lighting a candle says *yes* to warmth, heat, and self-care. It even gives a sense that there's help somewhere nearby, perhaps in another dimension.

You will always be rewarded when you focus a part of your atten-tion on the body's needs while you do your work in the world. Much more will get done than if you were driving yourself grimly against pain, fatigue, or tension.

My own experience—when recent dental surgery left me hurt and exhausted—with a deadline I was forced to meet, was that I lost touch with my Body Being. I slogged along as the pain got worse. Finally I set an alarm to go off every hour, stop what I was doing and sit down for five minutes to focus on slow breathing.

"How do you feel?" I would ask the healer within. "What would you like me to do right now?" The suggestions that appeared in consciousness always pointed to some form of relief. When I gave them the time they needed I was often able to get back to work.

Tai Chi and Qigong masters remind us that *chi*, the creative energy of the universe, is naturally present in and around us to sustain health and promote recovery. Master T.T. Liang told me that the word *relax* was an inadequate translation of the Chinese *sung*. He explained that what's important is a loosening of the muscles, a release of tension, as you give up external muscular energy in order to preserve your internal energy.

Master Cheng Man-ch'ing calls it energy conservation. He says you are learning "to throw every bone and muscle of the entire body wide open without hindrance or obstruction" so the *chi* can pass through. The *chi* is the healer. It just needs some help from the mind's attention to enhance the healing process. To understand better how to collaborate with it, let's turn to the next step, **Grounding Yourself on Mother Earth**.

Grounding Yourself on Mother Earth

Accessing the Healing Power of Earth
"To touch the earth is to move into harmony with nature."
Oglala Sioux

Shamans, Native Americans, and wisdom teachers all over the world see the earth as a giant, conscious, living being. They say pollution sickens her in the same way cancer spreads slowly through a human body.

Debilitated though she may be, our Mother Earth still retains tremendous power to heal. When we physically ground ourselves on her surface we are gifted with her vital energies.

The science behind it is simple: The water in your body acts as an electrical conduit to earth's negative ionic charge so you feel better when any part of you touches it. Charged particles that come originally from the sun reach the Earth in lightning, electrifying its entire surface. And while lightning may not be flashing across the sky right where you are, it's always flaring somewhere, creating a continually flowing current from the ionosphere to the earth.

James Oschman explains that "From the top of your head to the earth's surface, there is a potential you don't feel, because it doesn't cause any particular current to flow, even though it can be a couple of hundred volts. And depending on the changes in weather, that potential can go up from a hundred to 10,000 volts per meter."

As your bare feet make direct contact with the earth's energy field, your body becomes equalized to its energy level or potential. That will gradually synchronize your internal biological clocks, hormonal cycles, and physiological rhythms.

For more on Oschman's investigations, turn to his groundbreaking books, *Energy Medicine: The Scientific Basis,* and *Energy Medicine in Therapeutics and Human Performance.* He and others at the forefront of research into alternative healing solutions invite us to enter into a deeper dialogue with mind and body and take more responsibility for our own mental and physical health. You can also look into continuing research at the Earthing Institute to stay up to date on how access to earth's energy can keep you healthy and vigorous.

It was Clint Ober, a retired cable TV executive, who figured out that ever since people have worn synthetic-soled shoes, their bodies have been insulated from the same energy field that stabilizes not only cable TV but all industrial and residential electrical equipment throughout the world. He wondered whether the human body might benefit from similar grounding.

And he was right. Our immune system functions optimally when our body has an adequate supply of earth's free electrons—the antioxidants that are a major weapon against disease.

However, since you can't go barefoot outside all the time, various conductive systems have recently been developed that can ground you indoors to the same electrical charge as earth's surface while you work or sleep. An *earthing* sheet for your bed allows you to absorb electrons throughout the night, or a mat under your bare feet can ground you while you work at your desk.

Acknowledging Your Living Matrix
"Humankind has not woven the web of life. We are but one
thread within it. Whatever we do to the web, we do
to ourselves. All things are bound together . . .
all things connect."
Chief Seattle

Based on his studies in biophysics and cell biology, Oschman envisions the body as a web, a semi-conductive fabric that connects everything in the body, including the inside of every cell. He calls this system a living matrix, and describes it as "a continuous and dynamic 'supramolecular' webwork extending into every nook and cranny of the body; a nuclear matrix within a cellular matrix within a connective tissue matrix."

That means every time you touch a human body you are making contact with a continuously interconnected system, composed of virtually all of the molecules in the body linked together. Since what happens in one corner of that system will affect all the others, the properties of the whole net will depend on the integrated activities of all of its parts.

This whole fabric—you—is, in fact, an antioxidant defense system. If you go barefoot, your body will take in and store earth's electrons because we contain what's called *ground substance*—a gel-like material that hoards electrons and is part of our connective tissue.

What's more, the earth-based electrons that enter your feet can move anywhere in your body. Wherever a free radical forms, they can neutralize it and prevent mitochondrial damage, cross-linking of proteins, and mutation or genetic damage.

While it sounds miraculous, there is plenty of science behind it. Grounding to Mother Earth balances the immune system and reduces pain by altering the numbers of circulating neutrophils and lymphocytes.

It also affects various circulating chemical factors related to inflammation—the primary cause of many diseases. "Inflammation, which in medicine is considered an important part of the healing process, is really an artifact caused by lack of electrons in your tissues," Oschman explains. "The neutrophils deliver the free radicals to the site of injury in what's referred to as an oxidative burst.

"They are like Pac-Man—very important molecules that tear things apart. If bacteria have entered through your skin, these free radicals will destroy them very quickly. If you have damaged cells, the free radicals will break them apart so that there is a space for healthy cells to move in and repair the tissues. But in so doing, some of those free radicals can leak into and damage healthy tissue."

Not to worry however, because free radicals are positive and electrons are negative, so sooner or later any free radicals that leak into the healthy tissue will be neutralized.

Candace Pert, herself a medical research pioneer, celebrates Oschman's new vision of the human body as "a liquid crystal under tension, capable of vibrating at a number of frequencies . . . a dynamic, shape-shifting bundle of multiple personalities . . . capable of sudden and dramatic transformations."

Now *that* is hard to visualize! How can this body, with its firm bones and soft flesh, be a liquid crystal? We ordinary folk have only recently begun to wrap our minds around the new physics, doing our poor best to imagine a solid wooden table as a nest of swirling atoms and molecules that a karate chop of intention could break in half.

But Oschman clarifies: "When we think of crystals, we think of hard mineral crystals such as diamond or agate. The living crystals within us are made of long, thin, flexible molecules that are packed together in regular arrays, like the atoms of mineral crystals, but soft and flexible."

To invite those healing electrons into your living matrix, all you have to do is stand with bare feet on the ground (or buy a grounded sheet for your bed, a pad for your feet, or patches for the balls of the feet). "Grounding or earthing protects your body from what I call collateral damage," adds Oschman. "Damage that was not intended to take place but happens because we have disconnected ourselves from the Earth by putting rubber and plastic on the bottoms of our shoes."

Emerging new electromagnetic devices to lessen pain and cure wounds go far to confirm this new vision of the human being as a living, moving matrix of electromagnetic forces forever in play, as body and mind continually readjust to whatever's going on in and around us.

If this all sounds far fetched to you, wait till you are feeling stressed out or coming down with a minor ailment. Then go outside and stand barefoot on the ground for 10 or 15 minutes. Having done it myself many times, I guarantee you will soon begin to feel better.

Investing in the Ultimate Anti-Aging Strategy

"Heart disease and diabetes, which account for more deaths in the U.S. and worldwide than everything else combined, are completely preventable by making comprehensive lifestyle changes. Without drugs or surgery."
Dr. Dean Ornish

Free radicals are also a central issue in aging, causing damage to the body through injury, chronic inflammation, poor breathing habits, and the food we eat, among other things. So a healthy balance of antioxidant electrons to free radicals sounds like just what the doctor would order.

And he does. Stephen Sinatra, a cardiologist certified in anti-aging medicine and nutrition, is also an expert in energy medicine. He tells us that earthing may enhance the production and recycling of adenosine triphosphate (ATP) in our bodies. That will improve the functioning of our cardiovascular and immune systems, and slow down the process of aging by the same principle underlying metabolic cardiology.

Since ATP is the body's primary energy source, our bodies take electrons from fatty acids in order to recycle it. While Sinatra acknowledges that more research is necessary, it seems that when we absorb negative free electrons from the earth's surface, they may recycle ATP more easily.

So I asked him what effect does earthing have on the world's number one killer—cardiovascular disease? He says that, for one thing, recent tests indicate that grounding thins your blood, reducing viscosity and clumping. This is important because just about every aspect of cardiovascular disease has been correlated with elevated blood viscosity.

Dr. Sinatra's research team has measured it using a method called *zeta potential*, which quantifies the potential on your red blood cells by determining how fast they migrate in an electrical field. It turns out that when you ground yourself to earth's frequency your zeta potential quickly rises, which means your red blood cells have more charge on their surface, forcing them apart from each other.

This causes your blood to thin and flow more easily and your blood pressure to drop.

What's more, because they repel each other, red blood cells are less inclined to stick together and form a clot, and therefore less likely to form a pulmonary embolus. In other words, if your zeta potential is high through grounding, not only does the probability of heart disease decrease, but also your risk of multi-infarct dementia, which leads to loss of brain tissue from micro-clotting in the brain.

Because of all this, Dr. Sinatra likes to call grounding *Vitamin G.* As one of his scientific studies concludes: "Grounding appears to be one of the simplest and yet most profound interventions for helping reduce cardiovascular risk and cardiovascular events."

There's further good news for those of us who seek a youthful-looking face. In a 2014 study led by Gaétan Chevalier, a scientist in the Developmental and Cell Biology Department of the University of California at Irvine, his team found that earthing improves facial blood circulation and flow. The report concludes: "Even one-hour contact with the earth restores blood flow regulation to the face, suggesting enhanced skin tissue repair and improved facial appearance."

Receiving Earth's Gift
"Earth's crammed with heaven . . . But only he who sees takes off his shoes."
Elizabeth Barrett Browning

The simplest way to practice earthing is to take off your shoes and walk on the grass. Another ideal location is the beach. But if you want earth's precious electrons to gift you with good health, avoid asphalt and wood, as well as typical insulators like plastic or rubber.

"Earthing is the easiest and most profound lifestyle change anyone can make," says Oschman. "The moment your foot touches the earth, or you connect to the earth through a grounding wire, your physiology changes. An immediate normalization begins, and an anti-inflammatory switch is turned on."

City dwellers like me must seek out parks for barefoot walking. And we can buy earthing sheets to ground ourselves indoors for a really good night's sleep. The brick wall in my study—part of the original foundation of the building I live in—goes straight down into the earth. So I sometimes rest my hands or forehead against it to absorb negative electrons when achy joints make themselves known. Concrete is also a good conductor as long as it hasn't been sealed (painted concrete doesn't allow electrons to pass through).

As for those who seek the luxury of a penthouse, Oschman suggests they think twice: the higher you are above the earth the weaker the power of grounding. He predicts that those who live nearer the top of a high-rise will have more health issues than the people who live on the first floor.

Personally I have found hands-on cooking a rewarding experience—cutting, peeling and slicing with my own hands, rather than using machinery to do it. Touching raw food contacts earth energy, just like digging, planting and caring for flowers in my small window boxes. It also offers one more reason to cook for oneself and leave those processed foods behind.

Another source of nature's bounty comes from contact with animals. When in a state of stress, I cuddle my cat in my arms. Tension, anxiety and indigestion gradually quiet down as the rest-and-digest part of my nervous system takes over and deep breathing begins. So if you have a cat, dog, or horse, hug it often.

Finally, it will come as no surprise that earthing helps us feel better emotionally. Dr. Chevalier's recent study on earthing's effect on mood improvement (Ammons Scientific Psychological Reports-April 2015) concludes that "grounding may be a simple way to improve mood states and help mitigate common detrimental effects of negative moods on health and psychological state—such as anxiety, stress, and depression."

Take a few minutes to meditate on the intimate connection between your own nature and Mother Nature. Here's how John Muir calls up that intimacy of Being: "The sun shines not on us but in us. The rivers flow not past, but through us. Thrilling, tingling, vibrating every fiber and cell of the substance of our bodies, making them glide and sing. The trees wave and the flowers bloom in our bodies as well as our souls, and every bird song, wind song, and tremendous storm song of the rocks in the heart of the mountains is our song, our very own, and sings our love."

Settle down into yourself for a few minutes until any automatic nervous activity quiets down. Then imagine that you are an ocean. As a large body of water you contain many things, both small and large. Some of them are organic—life forms of different kinds.

Many are beautiful and/or friendly, but some are too dark, ominous or big for anyone to feel comfortable near them. There are valuable objects floating around within you, made with thought and care. But also a lot of flotsam and jetsam—like the islands of plastic garbage that now inhabit the world's oceans.

All of this moves within you—call it your *inner life*. But you are the ocean itself, so you don't need to do anything about it. You just allow everything a place in you, even though you may sometimes wonder where it came from and what use it serves.

As the winds and the seasons move above and around you, sometimes forming towering waves, other times scarcely wrinkling your smooth surface, you remain wholly receptive.

Sink your imagination deep into this image as you experience the waves at the top and the tides that pull secretly below. Begin to acknowledge that there is a stability in you that contains all things. Follow your breath as it comes and goes in rhythm with the waves. When you are ready to finish, ask yourself, "Who is at the center of this teeming life?"

Unloading the Burdens You Carry
"Nothing of mine is burning there."
Emperor Akbar

Do you have trouble letting go of the past? Do you hold on to objects that meant something to you back in the day, or attitudes that seemed like a good point of view at the time? How about things done or left undone that still burn a hole in your heart? Whether you dwell on the high points of days gone by or keep negative reactions and sorrows alive, you are stuck in the past.

Meanwhile, life both outside and inside you is in constant movement, from the flow of oxygen-rich blood that nourishes the body to the flow of impressions that feed the soul. To live within yesterday's habits and comforts without taking any risks denies the full experience of our present life.

But how to let go of yesterday's regrets or tomorrow's dreams in order to be nourished by today's life-energy? If the Buddha had it right, it's "the hankering and the dejection" that have us all in thrall. Maybe you could put less energy into wanting things. Then, if you are able to accept a wintry time of readjustment, the promise of rebirth will become as real as the inevitability of spring.

The first step is to see just how tightly you hold on. Notice your thoughts and feelings whenever past wounds or successes visit you during the day. Write them down like a scientist noting details of an experiment. At the end of the day, fit them into general categories, giving a name or a color to each category. Become aware of internal mutterings like: "Nobody understands." "They made me mad." "Wow, that turned out well!" "I wish I hadn't said that." "He has no right!"

How about last night's dreams? Are they still mesmerizing you? Or are you still grumbling about the creep who bumped against you in the subway? How did you feel when everyone stopped talking the minute you came into the ladies' room? Place any resentments or reactions into your categories. Experience how they interfere with the possibility of living in the present.

Ask your inner scientist to make a detailed list of whatever unresolved cargo you are carrying right now, and mark with an asterisk what you might be getting ready to let go of. Include everything in the inner refrigerator where you store up resentments or bad feelings about yourself or others.

Which do you hold onto longer, resentments of others or bad feelings about yourself? Write it all down. Then look for what triggers these feelings. Maybe there's a button others press that never fails to activate a negative reaction in you. See if you can find it and deactivate it.

Change is hard. Remind yourself that *seeing* comes first, long before making changes. Even if you feel it is a long way home to your True Self, you are following the path that leads you there. Then, if you are still trudging along with a heavy backpack and large rolling suitcase of needs and problems, consider building a mental raft to float your burdens alongside you on the river of life. That way you could walk along beside them with a lighter step.

When I looked in the mirror this morning, I saw a furrowed brow, and had to laugh. Since nothing big was weighing me down, why so fraught? *So* I asked myself, "Exactly what is the load you carry?" My first thought was Duty—what life calls me to support and what I *ought* to do. Do *oughts* and *shoulds* have you in thrall too? Then there's Longing—what I want and the discouraging feeling that I'll never get where I want to go. Familiar? Finally I recognized my Neediness—side by side with a wish to be true to myself.

Perhaps you too feel the weight of these three, all tied up in our rules-to-live-by. Do you have to win the race, pass the test, be successful? Do you desperately need to be liked, and seen for the complex, interesting person you are? And must you hide your tears and avoid expressing your emotions so as not to rock the boat or feel shame?

If you can acknowledge some of the unconscious drives that dominate your responses to life, you will begin to create an alternative narrative. Open a conversation with yourself, which could go something like this: What would happen if I stopped thinking of duty as burdensome? Might it then be a service to a higher purpose or to those I love?

As for longing, if I could give up wanting to be what and where I'm not, perhaps I'd free myself from a heavy weight. Then, were I to sacrifice my *angst* for a perfect life sometime in the future, maybe I'd discover the joy of being present to the only real time I've got.

Finally, if I could accept that the most important thing in life is relationship, I could begin to break down the barrier between me and everyone I fear might hurt me. At that point I might discover that 'i' is really we and that the energy I seek comes from our mutual support—the community of human beings. Love is an energy that flows through us all, like that river you can never step into twice.

Which brings me back to the question, why so fraught? What did we expect from life, more than we're getting? Perhaps we assumed we knew the rules we should play by until we discovered it was a different game. Think about Akbar, Emperor of India, standing on a nearby hill watching his enemies loot his town and set his palace aflame. Could we too surrender some of our earthly importance and worldly goods in order to get on with our life, broken though it may be?

We can't all be as inwardly free of identification as he was, so don't let that discourage you. Open to help. Imagine that you are cutting through the jungle of acquired fears and burdens with your machete as you seek a way out. There you are, trudging along day after day after day in the shadow of the huge trees, endlessly nervous about hidden dangers and under attack by biting insects.

Suddenly you perceive an open space ahead. You perk up. There you are, on the sunny bank of a huge river, filled with joy for a moment, thinking you've arrived. Oops. Your head and heart droop as you look across the water and see that there's nothing but more jungle on the other side. All this effort for nothing!

But wait a moment. If you take a more careful look at the other bank, perhaps with your heart in your mouth, you will see that, on the other side of the river, someone has been cutting a path towards you!

This metaphor I heard from Marion Woodman always gives me goose pimples. It may be hard to accept in this broken world, but it's true. We are never alone. We are always met. There is always help if we open to it.

So if you are weighted down by past and present burdens, think about letting them float along on a raft beside you as you follow the river of your life. It will probably sink someday and you will be free.

Coming Up From Below

*"If we could surrender to Earth's intelligence, we would rise
up rooted, like trees."*
Rainer Maria Rilke

Alexander Technique teachers tell their students that we humans
are blessed with three pairs of feet: the ones we stand and walk on,
the sit-bones on which we perch when sitting, and the tiny protu-
berances of the skull that allow the head to ride freely on top of the
spine.

While all three point downward in the direction of the gravitational
pull of the earth, it's a fascinating fact that the more attention you
can bring to these three sets of feet—sensing your weight as your
feet sink into earth, noticing how your sit-bones settle into the chair,
or how your head rides delicately on top of the spine—the more
aware you will become of an equal and opposite energy that surges
up through you from below.

Conscious kinesthetic awareness—attention to where you are in
space—awakens this sense of two energies moving through you,
one flowing down through the bones in obedience to the law of
gravity and the other streaming upward in response. While most of
the time you are probably quite oblivious to both as you go about
the business of living, every time you turn your attention to these
two currents of energy the unnecessary tension you carry will begin
to release.

When you open to the experience of the energy coming up from
below simultaneously with the energy coming down from above,
you stand between two worlds, nature and spirit, earth and heaven.
You are present to both of them. In *Inner Yoga*, Hindu teacher Sri
Anirvan offers a powerful image of beautiful Shakti, who represents
matter and the Feminine Principle. She lies curled up deep inside
each of us, sound asleep, until Shiva, or consciousness, whose
Being is spread out everywhere in the universe, sends down a ray
of light to awaken her.

Imagine how startled she is! Full of joy at the summons, she raises
her arms upward to receive his embrace. Anirvan says that each
time we focus conscious thought on our bodies, the gulf between

matter and consciousness decreases. A new level of consciousness is created.

In Jewish mysticism *Shekinah* is one of the names of God, rooted in the Hebrew word for *dwelling* or *resting,* and defined in the *Encyclopedia Judaica* as "the Divine Presence . . . the numinous immanence of God in the world." As soon as we gather into our Body Being the energy and attention dissipated in continual over-reaction to life's stresses, we open ourselves to the presence of God in the world, the union of body, soul and spirit.

"The things that happen to me day after day, the things that claim me day after day—these contain my essential task," says Martin Buber. "All contain a mysterious spiritual substance which depends on us for helping it towards its pure form . . . Man was created for the purpose of unifying the two worlds."

You can practice *coming up from below* through yoga, Tai Chi, Qigong or other exercises that lead to Body Consciousness. Any time you walk somewhere you could focus on the sensation of your feet caressing the ground. Or you could learn to stand like a tree as you send the mind a full-bodied invitation to join the dance of cells and neurons.

Standing Like a Tree
"You are a miniature field of the electromagnetic energy of the universe."
Lam Kam Chuan

The ancient Chinese rituals of Tai Chi and Qigong offer exceptional ways to work on connecting this earth energy, our vitality, with heaven energy—innate intelligence or wisdom. An essential part of this practice is to focus on the body's center of gravity, a couple of inches below the navel and deep within the belly. In China it is called the *lower dantian, elixir field,* or *sea of chi.*

Gurdjieff has referred to this place as the center of gravity of our Being, saying that it supports our thought and feeling as well as the whole upper body. According to Jeanne de Salzmann it is main-tained by our search for sensation, which she calls "an act of Presence." From this center of gravity she assures us that, "in a wholly natural way, I can stay in contact with all the parts of myself."

Stand Like a Tree or *Zhan Zuang* can be practiced anywhere, with or without a teacher. Stand with your feet shoulder-width apart, focus on the lower dantian, and release your weight into the earth as if your feet had roots like a tree.

Although invisible to us, a tree's roots spread out wide within the earth, providing both stability and nourishment. Visualize sinking your own roots deep into the earth as energy surges up into you like sap rising from below.

Gradually you will become aware of how your weight flows down through your bones in obedience to the law of gravity, as an equal and opposite surge of energy comes up from below. In fact, the response from below is always there—it's what keeps us upright—but unless we presence it consciously we are unaware of it. When we give it our conscious attention, we begin to feel its power.

As Jeanne de Salzmann points out, "The body obeys the attraction of the earth, from which it draws its energy. The subtle force, a finer energy in me, obeys another attraction . . . When I obey the earth's attraction in a conscious way, the subtle force is liberated and my ordinary 'i,' my ego, finds its place, its purpose." Then she adds a cautionary note, that thinking about it doesn't help because "I must live it."

Take a minute or two to ground yourself as you stand there. Then move your thought slowly from feet to ankles to knees. Are you holding tightly onto these joints in order to stand straight and not topple over? If so, soften your knees a little and allow the sacrum to drop naturally, as if you were perched on a huge beach ball.

Don't be alarmed if you begin to sway a little. That slight movement means you are ready to meet whatever comes your way with an activated Body Consciousness.

As you put your thought to work, imagine that your body is a work of art and your mind a slow-motion camera. Move its *lens* slowly up your legs and into the pelvis, chest, back, and shoulders, then down your arms to the hands. Investigate every nook and cranny to discover what state your different body parts are in.

Allow time for your body to respond to your mind's explorations. You will gradually become more aware of different pockets of tension in different places. Some muscular strain may even shift from place to place, just as your thoughts are always changing. Notice it as you stand there. Are there any constrictions you might be able to release simply by attending to them?

Finally, raise your arms to a horizontal level at the height of your shoulders in a hug-the-tree position, palms toward the chest. Release your shoulders. Allow the full excursion of your breathing—the quieting in-breath and the lengthening out-breath. Then break into a smile. Note how that lightens the heart and pelvis as the face muscles relax.

The first few minutes of *Stand Like a Tree* can be pretty uncomfortable, but if you stay with the effort a little longer you will begin to experience the rewards to come. You will feel less precarious, more grounded. Your breathing will deepen as you stand consciously between two worlds, your feet rooted in the earth, your thought focused on the center of gravity in the belly, and your head rising into the heavens.

In this position, poised between sky above and earth below, you represent *humanity* or *compassion* in the ancient Taoist ideal of *Zhen Ren* or *True Person*. Daoists believe that this *Primordial Stance* brings earth toward heaven and heaven toward earth. It invites the masculine and feminine forces into relationship with each other. Spirit or yang energy is associated with masculine, heavenly or creative energy, while the feminine yin is found in earth, body, matter, and nature.

Day and night, sun and moon, yang and yin endlessly play with each other. While yang energy gathers through the morning to dominate our actions by midday, it gradually cedes its authority to yin as light fades from the sky. Both are equally important. In fact, nothing moves except within the dance of *yin* and *yang*.

Master Lam Kam Chuen tells us in *The Way of Energy* that standing like a tree offers a renewed circulation of the original, natural energy in our bodies and minds. And master Yang Yang explains how important this exercise is for strengthening the body, growing the bones, and honing the mind. He says that when you stand still and relax all your muscles, your bones respond to this "effortless effort" by growing in density.

That means the five to ten minutes a day you commit to this practice could reverse osteopenia as well as help you regain a finer sense of balance. And there's an added bonus: he says that no matter what time of day you stand like a tree, you will sleep better at night.

Try it out anywhere you are forced to stand and wait—in line at the bank, waiting for the next bus, for the red light to change, or for someone to meet you. You need never wait impatiently again! Just focus your thought on the lower dantian in the belly, send your roots into the ground, and open to the sensation of energy moving through you in both directions until your turn comes.

You can deepen this experience by imagining that you are standing in a slow moving stream. Water is flowing gently around you and through you, literally filling your mind with Body Consciousness. To practice filling body with mind, turn to Step Four: *Quieting the Monkey Mind.*

STEP FOUR
Quieting the Monkey Mind

Emptying Your Cup
"Quiet the mind and the soul will speak."
Ma Jaya Sati Bhagavati

There's a Zen story about a Buddhist scholar who searches far and wide, eager to learn from the greatest Master. He finally finds him and arrives, exhausted, to sit at the wise man's feet. Seeing his agitated state, the Master offers him some tea, pouring from the pot until the cup overflows. The new disciple wonders if he's come to the wrong place. Is the old man a bit gaga? Nevertheless, he waits politely for clarification. "You come to ask for my teaching," says the Master. "But your cup is already full. Before I can teach you, you'll have to empty your cup."

What is our cup full of? Surely tons of information we've picked up along the way, both useful and unnecessary, plus any number of reactions, complaints, and longings. So when we look for help like the Buddhist scholar, hoping to contact a deeper level in ourselves, we are already full to the brim of the mind's agenda.

So if you seek some ideal inner Nirvana, you are standing squarely in your own path. Like all of us, the first thing you need to do is empty your cup. There are many useful exercises for this—counting the breath, repeating a mantra, or circulating the light. But if you have already experimented with many of them, sometimes it's best to just *stop trying anything*.

For example, you might tell yourself, "I am Earth. Heaven lives and moves in me." Then experience the small piece of Earth that you are. Focus on the sensation of yourself sitting there, arms, legs, belly, torso—a breathing being with much still to learn. Then wait patiently for a wave of Body Consciousness to spread through you. It may come from above, from below, or from the silence itself.

The absence of patience is part of our problem. Why are we always so busy, never allowing ourselves time to tune into our own inner world? Like the disciple's cup, our life fills up with our demands on it and its demands on us. Do you think you have to hurry because everyone else is faster and knows better what they are doing? It's not true. They are hurrying as fast as they can, just like you and me.

Pulitzer prizewinning reporter Charles Duhigg, author of *Smarter Faster Better*, says, "Many people feel like they're not fulfilled and not satisfied because they feel completely overwhelmed by what they're being asked to get done every single day." He urges people to contemplate more *why* they do what they do, to make choices rather than react to the demands that come at them.

Don't be taken in by the false assumption that work is hard or boring, and 'play,' or sitting around with your feet up, is good for you. "You're not happier because you turn your brain off," says Duhigg. "You're happier because you encourage yourself to think more deeply about what actually matters." Wise men have been telling us that for years. Surely it is time to listen.

For example, you could create some room in your active day for mini-moments of intentional communion with yourself. Each time you get up from your chair is a chance to stop and stand still for an instant and ask yourself why you are doing whatever you are about to do. A coffee or tea break offers an opportunity to pull your thoughts consciously away from your worries or duties for just a few minutes as you listen to the sounds of your own Body Being.

Your practice begins as you focus your attention on your intention, whether seeking to empty yourself, listening to your inner world, or simply noticing the sounds coming from the world around you.

You might even set an alarm from time to time in order to come to a complete stop in the middle of your busy day. Then look to see how full you are of whatever's going on at that moment—worries, duties, reactions, longings—and clear some of the debris out of your cup.

As you commit to taking mini-breaks from the stimuli in and around you, those moments of self-awareness will begin to connect with each other. You begin to create a space that frees your mind and calls you back home.

Coming Down from Above

"While the left half of the brain does all the talking, the right half of the brain carries the music of experience."
Bessel van der Kolk

We spoke in Step Three of *Coming Up from Below*, and engaged the right side of the brain and the power of image in order to develop a conscious sensation of the Body Being. Now let's activate the left hemisphere to learn more about how the brain works. As you will discover, the power of the image rules here as well.

In *The Master and His Emissary: The Divided Brain and the Making of the Western World,* psychiatrist Iain McGilchrist writes that we attend to the world in two ways at once. That's because each hemisphere processes reality differently.

Let's unravel this a bit. As we've always thought, the left is primarily concerned with what it knows. Directed and focused, it thinks in abstractions and breaks wholeness down into parts, categorizing and making the world familiar. The right brain connects more with our experiences. It is receptive to sensory impressions, processes our emotions, and helps us see things in context and in images.

McGilchrist explains how the two sides of the brain process our life: "In the right brain we experience . . . the live, complex, embodied world of individual, always unique beings, forever in flux, a net of interdependencies, forming and reforming wholes, a world with which we are deeply connected. In the left we experience . . . a represented version of it, containing now static, separable, bounded but essentially fragmented entities, grouped into classes, on which predictions can be based."

Have you figured out yet who is the Master here? McGilchrist insists that the right hemisphere is the *master* and the left the *emissary.* Why? For starters, the right is primary in childhood, allowing you to see in a whole way and in relationship with other things. It provides meaning, embraces paradox, and makes possible what he calls "the *presencing* of the new." It turns out that the possibility of *presencing* will depend on whether both hemispheres are able to harmonize your view of the world before the left steps in to reduce everything to what it already knows.

As McGilchrist explains it, "the work of division having been done by the left hemisphere, a new union must be sought, and for this to happen the process needs to be *returned to the right hemisphere* . . . Real wholeness involves a balance between the hemispheres— between the two worlds *after they are differentiated*." That's an important distinction. The Emissary does the naming and organizing, but then must return to the Master Hemisphere to reconnect with the whole for deeper understanding.

McGilchrist relates the right hemisphere to affirmation and the left to denial. He says that when the two halves of the brain work together appropriately a third state appears—that of *presencing*.

Gurdjieffians will be struck by the similarity to the Universal Law of Three—a central pillar of the Gurdjieff teaching. It posits that every action, event or phenomenon results from the combining of three forces—positive and negative energies that oppose each other, and the Neutralizing Force that reconciles them.

And Dr. Jung emphasized the importance of holding the tension between the opposites so that the third or Transcendent Function can appear. The work of all three men—two of them giants of 20th century thought—confirms that when two opposing forces, ideas, or felt experiences are lived *at the same time*, a new state is awakened. Perhaps it is the state of *I AM*.

One way to access such a state by coming down from above is Qigong master Robert Peng's meditation exercise, *Under the Waterfall*. Imagine that you are sitting on a big flat rock in the middle of a running stream as the sacred element of water flows down on your head. Relax and allow it to wash away impurities, mistakes, anger, even sorrows.

Let it pour down "over your skin, muscles, blood vessels, meridians, nerves, internal organs, and your bones and bone marrow," invites Peng. In *The Master Key*, he offers many images and exercises to awaken a harmonious relationship between body, mind, and heart by coming up from below or down from above.

Practicing Beginner's Mind
"The mind uses the body and its brain along with our
relationships with each other, and with the
planet, to create itself."
Daniel Siegel

Daniel Siegel likes to open a conference with the question, "Does mind exist?" He isn't satisfied by the scientific definition still held by many today, that the mind is what the brain does, which he says essentially reduces the mind to an MRI.

His own definition: "The mind is an embodied and relational process that regulates the flow of energy and information." It emerges from both interpersonal processes and brain structure. "The brain is the social organ of the body, where one hundred billion neurons reach out to other neurons," he explains. "It is the firing patterns that lead, in part, to the experience of mind. There are two worlds—that of physical reality, and that of *mindsight.*"

In his book of the same name, Siegel defines mindsight as "our human capacity to perceive the mind of the self and others . . . a powerful lens through which we can understand our inner lives with more clarity, integrate the brain, and enhance our relationships with others."

Then what is the brain? Or "the embodied brain," as Siegel prefers to call it. At its most basic level, the brain is a nest of neurons in the head that connect our anatomy with our functioning as ten to the millionth power of firings take place. He says that our *neural firing intensity* is shaped by how we process our personal life experiences. It is a major key to how we are.

I asked him why, if neuroscientists insist we can change ourselves, we aren't more often at our best. He explained that while the brain can change states very quickly, the body isn't able to keep up with it. There needs to be a better relationship—a full partnership between them.

We could learn a lot from animals, he added, because their reactions dissipate quickly rather than festering and making them ill, as often happens with us. Think of a dog who slinks away ashamedly after a scolding, but soon returns wagging its tail, free of guilt or resentment, ready for whatever's next.

In his psychiatric practice Siegel emphasizes the development of secure attachment, mindfulness meditation, and effective psychotherapy, because they impact a recently discovered neural mechanism that promotes well-being.

"Now, for me, that's not a surprise," he says. "Because mindfulness promotes the growth of integrative fibers in the brain. Integration is the fundamental mechanism of self-regulation . . . Every form of change seems to require consciousness—education, parenting, personal growth. psychotherapy. Each of these ways we help others, or ourselves, to grow and change, to develop in a focused way, calls for the growing individual to be aware, to be conscious."

Mindfulness can help people regulate their internal states, including their immune system, their emotions, and their interpersonal interactions. Jon Kabat-Zinn, one of the founders of the Mindfulness Movement, tells us that, "In Asian languages, the word for 'mind' and the word for 'heart' are the same. So if you're not hearing *mindfulness* in some deep way as *heartfulness,* you're not really understanding it. You could think of mindfulness as wise and affectionate attention."

Everything that happens to you today—experiences, actions taken or not taken, thoughts that intrude or assist—is food for your life tomorrow. So if you want tomorrow to be more alive than today, open yourself to Beginner's Mind. Read Shunryu Suzuki's *Beginner's Mind.* Give up some of your expectations and see life freshly, as a child would. Practice intentional action.

Developing a Free Attention

"The only way to maintain and develop a free attention . . . is to have more voluntary contact, a conscious relation, with the other main functional parts of our being—that is, with the body and the feeling."
Michel de Salzmann

Each of us is endowed with a powerful instrument for change: our attention. So when you decide to focus it consciously, you are harnessing heavy-duty help—more powerful than any of us can imagine. It is a force that can create miracles.

Nevertheless, it must first be gathered, and in spite of our common illusion that we are in control, the intrinsic energy that could serve our aims and intentions is pulled away by any and everything we see or hear or think or feel.

The need for a new quality of attention is urgent, especially now that there is so much distraction everywhere we look. Simone Weil writes that the whole purpose of school for children is not so much to learn facts as to instruct students on how to gather their attention.

Alas, in Gurdjieff's parlance, our grandmothers forgot to teach it to us, in spite of the fact that it is our most important task. He offers an essential clue when he says, *"I am* where my attention is." Experiment with it at this very moment. Take seven deep, relaxed breaths right now, wherever you are, as you focus fully on your Body Being.

Neuroscientists emphasize the importance of a gathered attention both for our mental health and to stimulate more adaptability in the brain. Siegel compares coming down from above, or top-down processing, to a light that controls traffic. He invites us to discover our own internal green, yellow and red lights as we process whatever information comes at us.

Take a moment to make a list right now of the things, ideas, attitudes and people you tend to *green-light* or automatically find acceptable. Then note down where you often hesitate before rejecting or agreeing. In a third column you could list what you have categorically refused to accept.

The red-light list is especially important because it reveals how you limit yourself. Top-down thinking is useful when it helps to organize your life but becomes a prison if there's too much restriction. The truth is that no matter what limits we place on ourselves, the inner experience of world and self is flowing through us day and night.

Siegel explains how our moods and states within that flow are linked to anatomical changes in the brain. For example, he says that the experience of *presence,* which he defines as *attunement, resonance,* and *trust,* "increases telomerase, improves epigenetic regulation and enhances immune functions." He is convinced that presence is the door to integration because it improves both relationality and enzymes. Don't miss his powerful *Wheel of Awareness* meditation at *drdansiegel.com.*

As we become more conscious of who and how we are, we develop new neural connections. So as you discover more about yourself, invite more of yourself into your active awareness. Take Mary Oliver's message to heart: "This is the first, the wildest and the wisest thing I know: that the soul exists and is built entirely out of attentiveness." Then clear a space for the poet in you, or the soul, or even silence itself.

Turn your attention sometimes to listen to all your conflicting voices. At other times, assess your body's aches and pains with an eye to more self-care. And, whenever you can, open yourself to the deepest wish in your heart. In other words, try consciously to break away from anything and everything that may have held your attention hostage all these years.

Such *away* moments will connect you to the wish to be more present to your life. Gurdjieff recommends that at any moment of the day we check in with what's going on in mind, body and feeling at the same instant. He calls this "taking photographs." If you take a few snapshots of yourself in action every day, you will soon collect enough impressions of yourself *as you really are* to fill an album.

Bringing Your Mind to Your Movement

"Movement is life. Life is a process. Improve the quality of the process and you improve the quality of life itself."
Moishe Feldenkrais

Are you always in a hurry to finish the moves you need to make as you go through your day? I am. I push myself to fold my laundry fast, get a meal ready and wash up lickety-split. Or check my emails and answer them. Make "duty" telephone calls. Clean up after myself.

But think about it. This is our life we're hurrying through! If it's a path that's going to end some day in our final hour on earth, do we really want to hurry down it? It might just be worthwhile to taste every moment as if it were the last one. Experiment with that thought, even for one day.

Maybe because I'm getting closer to the last one myself, I've begun to enjoy tasks I used to hurry through—carefully folding my long scarf when I come home, and hanging up the jacket I used to throw down on a table near the door. I'd tell myself, "As soon as I get through the 'must do' list I'll have time for myself."

Don't get fooled by that whopper! Once I caught on to it, I began to argue with myself. "Dearie," I'd say (because I need a little affection as well as direction), "This moment right now is your time for yourself. *Your* folding time. *Your* straightening-things-up time. *Your* feed-yourself and clean-up-after-yourself time. There is no other time!"

That's my reality, and probably yours too. It's our life, inner as well as outer, that's engaged in whatever movements we make. If you really wish to be present, invite that reality into everything you do. Above all, *slow down*! Live each moment with affection. Treasure each movement you make. Treasure yourself. Even ask yourself out loud, "Just where am I going as I rush through the events of my life?"

The simplest way to connect with your own presence when you are busy doing what needs to be done is to bring your mind to the movements you are making. Yes, your thought is at work solving whatever problem is in front of you, but there's plenty of mind-room left to follow your movements.

Whether you are walking to the market or solving a problem about the wind sheer effect on the Golden Gate Bridge, focusing your mind on your movements develops the "muscle" of your attention. That's because every movement you make is, in fact, a 'whole-body' movement.

Test this out by visualizing for a moment the skin and fascia that cradle your bones and organs. You will discover that a simple turn of the head tugs at your body all the way down the spine to your coccyx. When you are standing, you might even be able to feel it right down to your heels. As you sense how each movement you make resonates throughout your whole structure as every cell adapts to the new positioning, it will enhance the quality of your work.

Even when you think you are sitting still, parts of you are always in movement. A drop of your blood pumped by the heart travels to the ends of your fingers or toes, then returns to the heart in a roundtrip that takes about one minute. Visualize the drop as it moves through a vast system of blood vessels—arteries, veins and capillaries more than 60,000 miles long—enough to circle the globe twice in a single minute.

To add to the activity that's going on under your radar, every part of your body responds at every moment to your thoughts and emotions—tensing, releasing, holding on, letting go. Bring your attention to sense both the tension and the spaciousness inside.

If you feel heavy after a day's work, you will indeed be heavier. Find relief from fatigue by visualizing yourself expanding to fill the room you are in, all the way to the walls. Or imagine you are soaring above the earth with the eagles. And if your hands are tired from all the work they have been doing, imagine that they are growing as big as baseball mitts.

If you have ever experienced a dangerous situation, you already know how mind and body bond instantly to interrupt any wandering thoughts or emotional reactions as they send urgent messages about time and space and where safety lies. Every inch of flesh, blood, bones and neuronal activity is suddenly available to get you out of trouble.

Such experiences are like no other, summoning one's complete attention to the present moment. But you don't have to be in danger to experience a concentrated mind/body connection. Become a disciple of the work you choose to engage in. Seek your own essential rhythm—a rhythm that is visible in the work of accomplished craftspeople all over the world as they sweep the floor, saw wood, paint a house, cook dinner. Their work, inner and outer, flows freely from their dedicated movements, for which daily, hourly, even momentary commitment is indispensable.

Embodying An Image
"I shut my eyes in order to see."
Paul Gauguin

A poet spends many years in a monastery. When his dear friend asks what he has gained, he replies that he has certainly been in contact with God but "I still don't know, am I a falcon, a storm, or a great song?"

This is an example of giving life to an image. We can feel in our bodies what Rainer Maria Rilke means, as if we were flying with a falcon above the ordinary world, raging or sorrowing in a storm of emotions or, quite the contrary, resting on the inner silence of a great song.

Poetry is a door to embodiment —heart food as well as mind food— because a great image, like a great idea, silences the monkey mind. Philosopher Gershom Scholem says that "The image escapes in every direction." It escapes our 'taking it in' with the head, which tries to wrap up and shrink the idea it stands for in order to 'grasp' it in a single dimension.

But an image contains many dimensions, stirring hidden parts of ourselves, calling on the heart to speak. It can be a mediator between the world of the mind, always busy following its own trails, and our search for Body Consciousness.

Psychiatrist Norman Doidge tells us in *The Brain That Changes Itself* how an image that surprises and touches us to the heart can actually alter our brain and transform the way we look at life. Such an experience causes plastic change, he asserts. It "travels deep into the brain and even into our genes, molding them as well."

In *The Genie In Your Genes,* Dawson Church encourages us to focus on positive images, thoughts, emotions and prayers—which he calls *internal epigenetic interventions*—because doing so will improve our health. "Filling our minds with positive images of well-being can produce an epigenetic environment that reinforces the healing process," he affirms, assuring us that when we meditate on them we are "bulking up the portions of our brains that produce happiness."

You have already felt the power of image when you focused on *Standing Like a Tree* in Step Three, poised between Mother Earth and Father Sky, feet deeply rooted in terra firma on which you live, move, and have your being. Each time you embody this primordial idea your physical, mental and emotional tensions release as you stand at the threshold of a deeper level of Being.

Many spiritual paths attempt to awaken mind and heart through imagery. Some recommend visualizing a holy being in order to merge with it for a little while. Or recalling someone you greatly admire and reminding yourself of what you value most in him or her.

Choose an image—perhaps from a photo, painting or sculpture—that reverberates in you. Set its likeness in the path of your everyday life. Put it up on a wall, a door, your chest of drawers, even your mirror. Meeting that image around any corner will reawaken you to your larger self.

However, if nothing comes to mind, evoke the image of the Sun God. You could even stand outside on a sunny day as you remind yourself that consciousness is everywhere—in the air we breathe, in nature above and below us, perhaps in every cell of our bodies.

Then focus on the place at the top of your head called the *fontanelle*—the soft spot you can feel on a baby's skull. Breathe out any stale air, stale thoughts and stale attitudes. Then breathe in through the fontanelle as you invite the rays of our brightest star to pour light and heat down into every nook and cranny of your Body Being.

Circulating the Light

"When the Light circulates, the powers of the whole body arrange
themselves before its throne . . . just as when the master is
quiet and calm, men-servants and maids obey his orders
of their own accord, and each does his work."
The Secret of the Golden Flower

From the point of view of the mind, the body is the vehicle, the house *"I"* lives in, the instrument that is *mine* to use. It serves me well or ill, and must be rewarded, wheedled or punished. From the point of view of the Body Being, the mind is the Director and supplier of solutions to its needs. But unfortunately it is also often the slave-driver or tyrant—disrespectful and ignorant of the extraordinary being it sometimes pushes around so thoughtlessly.

Nevertheless, they need to be *related*. Whether we seek to contact our authentic nature through stillness or in mindful movement, the searchlight of the mind needs to be turned toward our Body Being. The word comes from *relatus*, which means to bring back, refer back, or bring into connection, like a bridge.

The bridge between body and mind is made of attention, conscious attention. When *"I"* begins to perceive a state of muscular tension—or of heaviness when tired, or lightness when energized—your power of attention has built a momentary bridge between them. You are no longer lost in thought or submerged in how you feel. Gurdjieff would say two of your three *brains* have come together. A new possibility has come into play. You are two thirds of the way toward fully experiencing your own presence-on-earth.

For some of us this bridge is easier to build through conscious movement, while others find some form of meditation-in-stillness indispensable. If that is your case, there are many meditation exercises to center you. Zen masters suggest counting breaths; Hindus murmur mantras and visualize their gods; Christians engage in ritual and contemplative prayer; Muslims interrupt whatever they are doing to bow down to earth several times a day as they acknowledge a higher authority.

All these forms have a single aim: to quieten the monkey mind, silence our surface reactions, and unhitch us from the fixed attitudes that imprison the flow of our energy.

One meditation that has been helpful to me is the Circulation of the Light. You can read about it in *The Secret of the Golden Flower*, an ancient Chinese text that supposedly dates back to Master Kuan Yin-his, for whom Lao-tzu wrote his *Tao Te Ching*. It teaches us "to strengthen, rejuvenate and normalize the life-processes, so that even death will be . . . a harmonious ending of life." We are assured that whoever practices it can meet death as a conscious spirit.

The Circulation of the Light attempts to link the world below—the earth or animal level—with the world above, already within us. God, Allah, the Self, the Great Spirit, Chi, Universal Energy—whatever you choose to call that higher energy—is everywhere and in us. Only we are seldom related to it.

Through the power of consciousness—by engaging in self-questioning and developing an objective recognition of what is just and unjust—we can begin to experience our two natures, animal and divine.

The aim isn't to slough off the body and become pure spirit, but rather to engage in regular efforts that create and deepen a living channel of energy in ourselves so that spirit can incarnate in flesh and the two become one. Our mind must learn to anchor itself in the body.

Those who undertake this inner journey are advised not to give up their ordinary life occupation, because the purpose of this work is "To live in contact with the world and yet in harmony with the Light." However, we are warned that the ego will surely try to interfere: "If one wants to protect the primordial spirit, one must first not fail to subjugate the knowing spirit." The ego must accept to take second place so that the Heavenly Heart can become our "strong and wise leader."

Tai Chi master Da Liu taught me how to practice this meditation before engaging in Tai Chi practice. I sat on the floor in an erect posture and focused my thought-energy first on the lower *dantian*. Then, once thought had connected with a sensation in the belly, I would send mind-intention and chi down the front of the body, which represents the *yin* or "Functional channel," then up the back through the *yang* or "Governor channel" to the top of the head.

This *Microcosmic Orbit* begins in the belly, moves down and under to the coccyx, then slowly up the spine to the crown of the head. It rests a moment in the upper *dantian* or Third Eye in the forehead. From there it goes down the front to pause in the heart, and finally returns to the belly.

The Secret of the Golden Flower calls this circular course *fixation,* and the Light *contemplation.* The text then warns that "Fixation without contemplation is circulation without Light. Contemplation without fixation is Light without circulation." The energies of body and mind are equally essential to the opening of the Golden Flower.

Da Liu told his students they must practice "concentrated quietness" both in meditation, "in which the outside moves inside," and in Tai Chi practice, "in which the inside moves outside." Try for yourself to experience what he meant.

There are many ways to come down from above, bringing mind attention to embrace the body as Shiva embraces Shakti. Perhaps the most natural meditation of all is simply to settle down in your own small piece of earth, noticing, assessing, releasing, and waiting. Because within each of us is an inner guide who is ready to lead us if our ego concerns and psycho-physical tensions quiet down. As Gurdjieff has said, higher levels of mind and feeling are already fully developed in us. We just aren't yet open enough to receive them.

How to prepare our ordinary selves so that these higher energies can act on us? As you acknowledge your need at the deepest level, your tensions will release and your breathing deepen. Breath is a master key to Body Consciousness, so let's move to the next Step, *Breathing into Balance.*

Breathing Into Balance

Accepting Imbalance
*"Awareness is like the sun. When it shines on things,
they are transformed."*
Thich Nhat Han

Whenever you feel depressed, unhappy, or cut off from active participation in the world's work, it's time to re-evaluate the Body/Mind connection. Has body or mind become too foggy or too over-vigilant? Stormy weather may be coming your way. Or perhaps you're just headed away from where the winds of your life want to take you.

Truth is, balance is an ever-moving target. There is no fixed place inside that you could grab onto when you're wobbling, like a solid sofa-back. Four-footed creatures, down near the earth, are steady on their feet, thoughts alert for danger and centered on where their next meal is coming from.

But we upright humans are perpetually going off balance—sometimes tottering forward or reeling back, uncertain in body and stressed in mind about just where and how we are supposed to be. We need to pay more attention to our Body Being and the circumstances around us, as our roving ancestors did.

Nevertheless, manifestations of imbalance send a useful message. Any body-weave or stumble elicits a call from Central Intelligence to stop for a moment. Were you flying through the stratosphere on mental wings, cut off from your meat and bones? As soon as you realize that you were over-focused in thought or deep in emotional reactivity, ground yourself in the reality of the moment you are living through.

Let's define balance as a clear mind that sees and even foresees what's happening, a body that's tuned up and ready to engage in either action or repose, and an awakened heart. Steven Weiss says that "because we humans are spiritual beings inhabiting a physical body, the physical laws of the container exert a tremendous influence upon Spirit's ability to manifest in the body."

He points out that while conventional medicine essentially ignores structural integrity, spiritual healers are often ignorant of the laws governing the physical body. To return to balance, he suggests that we begin at the bottom like a good engineer who recognizes the primary importance of structural integrity for every weight-bearing system.

So when you feel unstable, you could reorient yourself by sitting down and taking off your shoes. Since your feet are stuffed most of the time into rigid, somewhat tomb-like structures, you can bet they will be enthusiastic to be free! Wiggle and squeeze your toes to say hello. Take each foot in your hands to palpate those twenty-six bones as they seek a right relationship with each other.

Then stand up and imagine a tripod at the bottom each foot, one of its feet at the center of your heel, another on the pad of the big toe and a third on the pad of the little toe. Remind yourself that the earth is coming up from below to support you so you can stop tensing to hold yourself up. If you locked your ankles and knees to keep yourself up, let them go.

Focus on your weight on the ground and turn your thought to the sensation of the flow of gravity down from your head, through the bones, and into the feet. As in *Stand Like a Tree*, you will soon experience an equal and opposite flow of energy upward from the center of the soles—a place on your feet called *Bubbling Spring* in Tai Chi, and *Kidney One* in acupuncture.

The force of gravity flows down through you. Earth energy surges up. As you attend to the movement of energy in both directions, you are *activating* the relationship between body and brain. There's a dynamic response in the body that's often called *toning* as oppositional forces begin to play with each other—between head and spine, spine and arms, torso and legs, legs and feet.

The next step is to *fire up* your whole system as you go into action. For example, take a walk. Note that because we habitually focus on where we are going rather than where we are, we always lose some support from the ground we are standing on. Instead, bring more attention to whichever foot carries your weight.

As an experiment, take a slow walk around your living room as you engage with weight and weightlessness. Attend first to the full sensation of your weight on the leg on which you are standing. Think of the weightless leg as empty. Then, as you step slowly onto it, gradually fill it up from the full one—measuring twenty percent, forty percent, sixty percent, and so on, until it is filled with your weight and the other leg is empty. Focus on the newly grounded foot as you lift the other leg and bring your weight onto it in the same way.

Whether you are going for a walk or standing around, life invites you to rediscover yourself both up and down, between earth and sky, by means of your conscious attention.

As you anchor the mind in your flesh and bones, and invite the heart to participate, your three inner worlds—head, heart, and body—come back into balance with each other. Herman Hesse could have been defining balance when he said, "We are a wave that flows to fit whatever form it finds." The form is already there. Fill it with mind.

Creating Conditions for Change
"You cannot live on gold you find in the streets.
You must mine your own."
G. I. Gurdjieff

In order to be the best I could be, I used to hope grace would descend from above to help me out. Finally I realized that the exchange between I and Thou is a partnership. Something is up to me in order for both sides to *appreciate* each other and work together.

Gurdjieff suggests that we create conditions that make a demand on us. That way our best effort will be required by the situation we are in, whether or not we are "in the mood." Maybe the demand will come through the job to be done, the person we are with, or perhaps from life itself.

In any case, because our habitual routines often put us to sleep, it's useful to place a stumbling block across the path of least resistance. Or you could think of it as jumping into a small frying pan as you light a small fire under it.

How to do this? Start by learning more about what makes you tick. The more you know about yourself the easier it will be to create conditions that press you to work at your best. Once alert to where your weaknesses are, your inner *sly fox* can figure out how to make demands on your everyday, hesitating, postponing self.

When the fire is lit and the inner witness is on the job to see that you carry through, your pride and honesty will help you meet the challenge with your best professional work. At that point, all the different aspects of yourself will come into play. The energies of Heaven and Earth, above and below, light and dark, will come together to support or dissuade you.

"Think what you feel. Feel what you think," advises Gurdjieff. In other words, if you want the energy of the universe on your side, bring intelligence, not just intellect, to the challenges you have created for yourself. Move forward connecting mind to gesture, movement to mind, and a heartful intention to both.

The minute you try, you will run into resistance. It's a cosmic law. Lao Tzu informed us that "the journey of a thousand miles begins with one step." What he didn't add is that each time we decide to live more consciously, we are once again right back at that first step!

It's a discouraging thought. Who wants to be back at the beginning when we always like to move forward. But if you focus mind and heart on the *aim* rather than the *obstacles*, you will be able to overcome the resistance. In any case, don't give yourself a gargantuan goal. Commit to what will put you on the spot but not overwhelm. Then choose to *respond* rather than *react*.

Neuroscientists advise us to cultivate the upper regions of the brain where greater neuroplasticity makes change easier. Rick Hanson points to the *anterior cingulate cortex*, which oversees attention, goals, and deliberate regulation of thought and behavior. It is in a unique position in the brain, with connections to both the *limbic system* where emotions rule and the *prefrontal cortex,* our frontal decision-maker.

When it brings *neural coherence* to an intention, we experience coming together toward an aim. Then our conscious will can both influence emotional reactions and be influenced by them—an indispensable exchange that integrates thought and feeling.

Here are a few experiments you might try: If you are as resistant to cleaning out your closets as I am, or need to get on with some other postponed task, why not light a small candle and accept to work until it goes out.

Or turn to Mozart on youtube, and let that great music accompany and lift your effort. Or set an egg timer and commit yourself to working till it goes off.

Or, if you have a job that's been lying in wait for a while, select something you very much want to do with a friend. You will go together only if and when you finish.

However, the concept of creating conditions to interrupt the status quo goes much deeper than the simple egg-timer level. By offering opposition to the habitual state of the moment you are literally inter-rupting the automaton—waking up parts of yourself that were asleep—in order to become more *real.*

So celebrate the positive effect of interruption, in spite of the fact that you find it annoying to be summoned away from the screen you are looking at, the book you are reading, the movie you are submerged in or the cabinet you are fixing. Practice conscious interruption.

Imagine a world in which the call to interrupt whatever one is fixated on comes five times a day. When the cry of the *muezzin* summons the Muslim world to prayer, everyone gives up the iden-tification with whatever they are doing to put their foreheads on the ground in the deepest of all possible bows. That movement puts the small self in its place for a moment, allowing another level of energy to occupy mind and body. First comes the interruption, then the deep bow, and finally the relinquishing of the busyness of the mind as it turns toward heartfelt thanks and grace.

A child or an animal is a perfect interrupter, often demanding your attention when you are totally engaged in something else, and refusing to take "Not now!" for an answer. My cat may nibble at my ankle when I'm deep in writing or even jump up on the keypad. Forced to take action, I could swat or scold her on the one hand, or turn away from my annoyance and play with her on the other. When I do that, I soon discover a fresher person has emerged to continue the work I was doing.

It's easy to get annoyed at such interruptions when they seem less important than what you are engaged in, but think of it this way. Here's a sudden demand for love that offers love in return. Refuse love at your peril! Receive the gift, take the dog for a walk, play with the child, and then return to concentrate on your important activities with new energy.

Celebrating Limitations
"Living within the limits that make my life my own."
Marion Woodman

Your far-ranging mind can take you anywhere in the world, but in the name of health and harmony you need to discover what is hemming the rest of you in. Whether your heart mourns its desolation or your mind its lack of meaningful work, knowing what limits you is crucial to re-establishing balance.

A major reason we are so dissatisfied is that we feel we aren't getting what we wanted from life. This hugely impacts our possibility to enjoy the life we have. An alternative path would be to sacrifice a few items on your list of requirements.

Write down a list of your 'needs' and try to give some of them up for a week. Limit a few of your demands on yourself, on your friends and family, and on life itself. Notice whether that impacts how you feel each day. What appears instead to fill the emptied space?

Accepting limitations includes allowing the body to move freely in space, unhampered by criticism or directives. Take time away from the automatic flow that goes on all the time as you think your thoughts and plan your plans. Instead, stay connected to your best friend as you make your bed, brush your teeth, fix your breakfast.

Hold back consciously from preparing and eating food quickly in order to hurry on to the next thing.

Another major limitation many people suffer from is loneliness, now recognized as epidemic in the Western world. A college teacher recently asked his students if anyone felt lonely. Immediately all hands went up.

Surprised, he asked the same question in his three other classes and the same thing happened. While experts say it's because we lack a meaningful relationship, could we be lonely because we lack an intimate relationship *with ourselves*?

Perhaps it is our inner life that needs our attention first. The fact is, if we wish to be more balanced—more wholly ourselves—we need to include more of ourselves into every living moment. So finding balance in the psyche is as important as avoiding a fall.

Begin to sense when you are closer to being centered in who you are and when you are playing a part. Take time to stay a moment longer listening to yourself when your heart aches. What is missing? In what way are mind and body off kilter with each other? If you want to explore this further you might find it useful to read Thomas Moore's *Care of the Soul* or Donald Kalsched's *Trauma and the Soul*.

Finally there's the mega-limitation of our multi-tasking world. We often complain that the body is too slow to do all we need to get done. Don't get caught in that one! The fact that your Body Being can do only one thing at a time is not a limitation but a huge blessing!

Celebrate the fact that while thoughts can soar and emotions can roar, your feet are subject to laws that keep them and you on the ground. Because every time you turn your attention on your Body Being, you come back to the *very moment you are living through*.

Return to the present moment right now, wherever you are sitting. Is your chair hard or soft? Do you feel stowed on it like a heavy package or are you perched lightly as a bird on a branch? No judgments. Just witness what *is*.

Now wiggle your fingers and bend them one by one, sensing the pull as they stretch at the joints. Then bow your whole upper body forward, releasing the spine little by little till your head almost touches the floor. Finally, as you roll back up, let your hands reach high above your head. Press your feet into the ground with hands still in the air and come up out of your chair, twisting like a rising cobra.

Feels good, you may say, but why bother? Because it is the simplest way to bring our busy head brain, our reactive emotional life, and this physical instrument of our being-in-the-world back into balance with each other.

Any time you find yourself bemoaning your inability to get your body to do what you want, make direct contact with it. You could even ask politely what it needs from you. Perhaps only a drink of water, or a moment to breathe freely, unfettered by your urgencies.

Why not entertain the possibility of a new and mysterious relationship between the *Me* you think you know, and the body you also don't know? For clearly, although you can go through life doing what you think you want as if you wholeheartedly approved of your decisions, there is a deep instinctive part of you that makes its own choices and has its own aims.

We do some things we love and love some things we seldom allow ourselves to do. Only when we accept our limitations and commit to a more intimate relationship between the mind and the Body Being will we come closer to the balance we seek.

De-Activating Stress
"Breathing is the body's natural way of restoring harmony."
Jessica Wolf

Stress, quite simply, takes us off balance. When under pressure we speed away from any hope of present awareness. First to succumb is the respiratory system. Breath held, ribs clutched tight, there's no longer a full flow of oxygen in and carbon dioxide out of our lungs. Lost is the full-bodied rhythm that includes the movement of chest and back as the diaphragm descends with the in-breath and ascends with the out-breath, massaging the heart and digestive organs.

The most important action you can take when you are feeling stressed is just to slow down. Make an effort to oppose the automatic, squirrel-in-a–cage adrenalin rush forward. To interrupt it, first acknowledge how hard it is to do. Then remind yourself how important it is for your well-being. You will be surprised at how much easier it will be to solve whatever problem or decision has you on the run.

In recent years, neuroscientists have been able to study the harsh effects of stress through observing on fMRIs the small changes in blood flow that occur during brain activity. They illustrate how our chronic rushing feeds anxiety and heightens adrenaline levels.

Like all our habits, stress builds up neural pathways that can grow in size from a footpath to a highway when repeated many times a day. As our brain gets hooked on stimulation, our bodies become addicted to rushing, and our minds switch to autopilot. Then, in spite of the fact that only a few tasks have true priority, everything seems equally urgent.

Here's one way to de-activate stress. Each time you are aware of feeling stressed, come to a full stop for a moment. Hold back your first impulse to go back into movement as if you were reining in a horse. That way you create a critical pause as you gather your attention. Then, once you are fully present to your state of tension, you can choose to move forward with more intelligence.

When you first try this, you may only notice how often you fail, because the urge to rush forward is so strong. But don't give up. Remind yourself that your neural pathways are not fixed. Your own efforts against the automatic flow of habits will transform them. Celebrate the new positive habit under construction! Give it a little more room each day.

Emotional stress pays a major part in knocking us off balance. There's a place in each of us that gets hit first and hardest by the blows of life. For me, it's always been the digestive system (*What is it in my life I can't digest?*). For you, maybe it's the upper back and shoulders or the lower back (*What can I no longer bear to carry?*). And who can stand firm with an aching pelvis, hips or knees (*I just can't stand this any more!*), or the pounding head that drives us to a dark, quiet room and away from what's unacceptable in our lives.

Every organ reacts to our emotions in its own way. For example, some people become breathless or discover a frog in their throat when they can't bring themselves to voice what they feel. Others may suffer from an inflamed liver due to repressed anger. Still others have kidneys and intestines that baulk at draining some of the waste out of the system.

Perhaps you've dreamt of toilets that won't flush, as I have. Or starving animals that look at you with anguished eyes. All of this is the body calling out to us. And the more urgent the situation gets, the more insistent the call.

But you are not helpless in the face of it. Your mind can help you negotiate the return to balance if you attend to the wounded part. Don't turn away, call it names, or accuse it of failing you. Accusations are truly counter-productive.

The body may not speak our head-language but it hears our accusations and reacts to them like an animal to a scolding. Instead, think of the suffering part of your Body Being like a child in need of comforting. She needs your attention and your thoughtful care.

Experiment with the following approach: start with acceptance. Rephrase whatever you were about to criticize yourself for by apologizing to the part of you that bears the burden of your attack. Try out a few new responses to messages of pain, fatigue or overwhelment like: "I'm sorry I've been overloading you with all my troubles." Or "let's take a break together."

Next you might do some research on herbs or treatments to help heal whatever area or organ is suffering. Take back pain, for example. It's scary to suddenly be barely able to move. But eighty percent of back pain is non-specific or use-related. Doctors can't find much that's wrong.

Sore backs respond to rest and heat, followed a few days later by gentle exercise. Lie on the floor in a semi-supine position for ten or fifteen minutes to release all tension and reassure your back that it doesn't have to carry more than it's meant to. Ask what it needs. Look more critically at what you insist on doing that is more than you/it can handle.

As for the pain in your joints—neck, shoulders, hips, knees, ankles and feet—much of it is stress-related. Which means it's not *what* you do but *how* you move yourself around with too much tension. One of the best methods to uncover poor habits of *use* is the Alexander Technique, a form of neuromuscular re-education that helps us regain the natural coordination and freedom we had as small children.

Take a look at the nearest toddler and you'll see a straight back, a confident step, and a body/mind filled with zest for exploration in spite of frequent totters or tumbles. We were once as freely up and away as they are, before our parents endlessly told us to sit up straight, our teachers insisted we stay in our chairs all day, or various physical accidents, ailments, and emotional demands created harmful habits of stress and tension.

While the Alexander Technique focuses on the chronic pain that stems from misuse, it helps relieve mental and emotional tensions as well. You learn how to move more freely whether you suffer from poor posture, arthritis, spine and joint pain, headache, tendonitis, carpal tunnel syndrome, or frozen shoulder.

The Technique can also help people cope with Parkinson's, multiple sclerosis, osteoarthritis, and other disorders of the musculoskeletal system. Musicians, actors, singers and dancers study it to perfect their performance.

F. M. Alexander's teaching developed from a study of his own difficulties, just as this book invites you to study yours. A young Australian actor, he began to lose his voice onstage, threatening his career.

When he looked at himself in a three-way mirror, he saw how the unconscious habit of tightening his neck to declaim his Shakespearian monologues was distorting his spine and causing faulty breathing. Eventually he figured out how to bring conscious attention to free his neck and lengthen his spine, and went on to share his discoveries with the world.

Moishe Feldenkrais was another brilliant mind/body innovator who developed his teaching to deal with a disabling soccer injury to his knee. An Israeli scientist and Judo master, he applied his knowledge of physics and engineering to body–brain mechanics, and went on to teach Functional Integration and Awareness through Movement.

Both Alexander and Feldenkrais called themselves teachers rather than therapists because they were teaching something their students could learn to do for themselves.

At the beginning you will need the help of a teacher's hands to uncover and release unconscious habits of excess tension, and learn practical exercises to restore a more balanced posture and coordination.

As your gentler, more thoughtful self discovers how you've put six times more pressure on your joints to sit, stand, walk, or lift your arms than is necessary, you will be amazed at how much easier it becomes to move around your world.

Getting Out of the Way
"Physical goes with spiritual the way front goes with back and up goes with down."
Rabbi Rama

In the summer of Steven Weiss' first year at medical school he spent time at the Zuni Indian reservation in western New Mexico and was eventually adopted into the Zuni Bear Clan. While there he witnessed the healing of an unconscious boy with a lurid bruise on his forehead by Zuni bone doctor Jimmy A'wa-sheh'.

After what seemed a miraculous cure—the bruise completely disappeared and the boy ran out to play—Jimmy explained to Weiss, "What more is a human being than just a bag of mud brought to this space by Great Creator to do the work of his ancestors? I just get out of the way! Great Creator comes through me; the spirits of my ancestors come through me and *they* heal, not me."

Weiss later studied with other healers including Reverend Rosalyn Bruyere, who told him that energy is all there is. He now approaches diagnosis and treatment with an eye to the human energy field, the chakra system, and Spiritual Law.

But he points out that before anyone can support healing, they must remove themselves and their filters so they can perceive without prejudgment or distortion. "Left to themselves, our eyes are doomed to see only what the mind knows," he explains. "By first getting out of the way we allow our eyes and hands to inform our brain."

In his own words, "Starting from a simple meditative state where I follow breath and heartbeat, I focus my awareness into the middle of my sacrum. Then I float that awareness, in the form of a small ball of light, out into space about eighteen inches behind my sacrum, freely suspended and automatically shifting. That's the state in which that ball of *chi* must remain.

"Then I fashion a single hook in space, again floating about eighteen inches behind the second sacral segment (middle of the sacrum). Next I peel off my attention as if I were pulling off a heavy winter cloak, and hang it onto this hook, freely suspended and automatically shifting, eighteen inches behind my sacrum."

He invited me to try this, and simply observe any changes in what I felt or how I perceived the world. "This is how I was taught to get out of the way—to allow Creator and my Ancestors to flow and work through me," he said. "However, whatever the 'it' is that we have removed and hung on that shifting hook behind us, you can be sure it doesn't like to stay there! It wants to slip off the hook and get back into my hands and brain, and create trouble. So my job is to keep it there on the hook when I am engaged in healing."

Weiss has honed this practice for many years and on many different levels. Now Medical Director of the Medicine Lodge Clinic and founder and educational director of The Altar of Creation, he practices healing based on what the body requires to find balance on both the physical or tissue level and the energetic or spiritual level.

"Energy precedes tissue," he says. "Does it initiate tissue or is tissue pulling energy? It's a dance . . . it's always changing!" He describes the *notochord,* or primitive core of the *embryo,* as a unique tissue that serves as a bridge between spirit and anatomy. It resembles a small flexible rod and is the *midline* in the early development of the embryo.

"This tissue, as our axis of creation, is at the core of our conscious-ness. It is the bridge between us and the breath of life," he affirms. "With its transformational, bio-electric nature, it's the basis of our ability to heal and regulate ourselves, the place through which we access the power and wisdom of what old-time healers called 'our body's memory of perfection' in primordial conscious-ness."

You can try his exercise as a meditative practice to calm the mind and support your own healing. But in order for the energy of cre-ation to heal you and those you love, you first need to hang that little guy who's clamoring for your attention out on that hook and keep him there for a while. The ego always wants to explain and control what's happening, give advice, or cheer on your spiritual success story. It must abdicate its authority and stop thinking it is in charge.

Start with no agenda. Send your thought in both directions as you connect bottom and top, head and coccyx, and just listen in. Return to the practice of getting out of your own way again and again. Over time the quality of your breathing and healing will shift more easily, and you will begin to *be* with yourself without being pulled away at every moment. Remember that the effort isn't to *do* something, but to become more *available.* You *allow* a new level of conscious-ness to access you.

Looking for Help in a New Direction
"We have in all naiveté forgotten that beneath our world of reason another lies buried."
C. G. Jung

How do you recover from crisis? Many of us turn away, grit our teeth, close our ears to any internal cries, and get on with whatever is next on our list. But what to do about the inner figure who enters our dreams at night without a by-your-leave, to disturb our present occupation and carefully laid plans?

Though we may think in our conscious mind that we know who we are and what we want, there's another energy that sometimes appears, seemingly alien to our own. It says, "Hey, You! Have you forgotten that I, too, am right here with you? I have my own aims and intentions. I, too, have a right to be *Me!*" (aka, you).

The truth is, our salvation from whatever present crisis we are in may lie in unknown parts of ourselves. Recall how such times were resolved in the fairytales of your childhood. An elderly king and queen live in a decaying kingdom, or under thrall of witch or dragon. Or a prince or princess (aka, the hope of the future) is mute, kidnapped or otherwise unavailable. Help is needed, but not even all the king's horses and all the king's men can save the situation.

Rather, new energy must enter. Where does it live? Sometimes it takes the form of a dwarf, a trickster, a bird, a colony of ants, or a youngest brother or sister no one ever noticed before. And don't forget how kissing the frog (ugh!) frees an enchanted prince. At some point in our lives we all confront a frog we can choose to kiss or not kiss.

In other words, you contain inner attitudes that may not view life the way your conscious mind does, and help may exist where you least expect it. Why not speak with the anguished or angry person in you, rather than distance yourself from him or her.

Inquire of the sufferer quite simply, "Why are you weeping?" (or fuming or feeling desperate). Or you might ask "Who isn't getting the attention she needs from me?" And "How can I help?" Then listen attentively, because the reply may come in a different form than you expect.

When this other world opens its doors, you will find that there's much more in you besides the conscious, busy person you know yourself to be. Perhaps some buried aspect of yourself calls out to you from the unconscious or from the soul, wanting to tell you something. Or perhaps some part of your *unlived life* is trying to get your attention before you leave the planet. Maybe some fragmentary *persona* is acting out whatever you have denied yourself. Wherever the energy coming from, you would do well to listen, and perhaps enter into dialogue with it.

Best to step carefully, as this *Other* may pursue quite different aims than those your conscious mind has signed up for. One of its characteristics, so unlike our usual way of being, is how it takes us by surprise.

We may settle in, dig ourselves a foundation for a particular way of living, and announce to the world that this is what I want, and that is what I stand for. But that Other may suddenly cry "enough!" and leave our intentions, our public persona, and our private image of ourselves blowing in the wind.

So if, like me, you are curious about these visits from another world within and game to explore it, here are a few ways you might catch a glimpse of what drives you where you may not want to go.

First and most important, ground yourself in your own physical reality. Think of it this way: if these are huge energies moving through us, we are safest when in touch with our own limitations and the small piece of earth we occupy.

Once you are ready to explore, begin to gather information about your emotional reactions like a scientist gathering data. No judgments about whether this or that was good or bad, just a description of what took place. Note any dreams or daydreams right when they occur. Next day, tune into whatever stirs you in them, without hunting too much for verbal interpretations.

Become alert to how differing attitudes rule you at different moments. When do you see yourself as the hero of your own romance, or the little match girl out in the cold, or an important public figure? When, with sorrowful pride, do you insist: "That's just how I am and I can't change!" And don't forget to write down any snide *sotto voce* comments you hear yourself make about someone else. What in you reacts that way to him or her?

Whenever you discover a heretofore unknown member of your inner cast of characters, you could begin to dialogue with it by gently asking it to explain what you don't understand. I have done this for many years, but I have to give up my in-charge self for a moment, because these hidden sides of us don't respond well to attitudes that challenge them. Why should they? How many know-it-alls would *you* want to open up to?

In other words, give up *knowing better*. You will then discover a powerful form of *deep listening*. When I asked my own inner tyrant why he was so harsh and accusing, he cried out despairingly, "Because you never listen!" The only way he could tell me something about myself that I didn't want to hear was by attacking me.

So if any answers to your questions come in the form of an attack, dodge the anger coming at you and ask that inner persona what it is *really* trying to say, aside from being critical and negative.

If no message responds to your queries, try painting your hurt, your anger, or your anguish. Just sit down in front of blank paper with a bunch of magic markers at your side and see what happens. Choose colors that go with your mood and let them roll wherever they want to go.

I once tried to paint the ugliest, angriest person I could imagine, and was astonished at the result—a beautiful Indian mask in bright colors. A primitive energy long hidden in my psyche had stepped into consciousness.

Painting, sculpture, poetry, music and dance can encourage the reappearance of inner fragments we may have marginalized since childhood because we were told they were bad. In fact, it is useful to reexamine old ideas of *wrong* and *bad*.

Yes, some aspects of our nature were put under conscious control for good reason, so we would grow up to be decent, civilized adults. But there are others we have refused to admit into consciousness through fear or wanting to *belong*—a wellspring of energy we may have locked up long ago in self-denial.

Engaging in The Action of Being
*"The mind is king of the senses, but the breath is
the king of the mind."*
Swami Svatmarama

Focus your attention for a moment on the inflow and outflow of your breath. Take a moment to imagine that you are at the seashore, lying on the warm sand as you watch the waves creep toward you and then slowly ebb back into the ocean. Your breath is like those waves, coming and going without your having to do anything.

Does your breathing deepen as you visualize this? Does your whole body begin to relax? A growing sense of expansion can be yours every time you tune in to your breathing. It is a master key to freedom from stress.

Attention to the breath is a practice common to many spiritual paths. For example, Sri Anirvan tells us that we contain three different currents of energy: the breath, the nervous system, and the flow of thought.

He says the mental current tends to be outer-directed, disorganized, incoherent, and easily dissipated. Nevertheless it moves in and out with our breathing, so we can steady our wandering or confused mind through focusing on the breath.

To do this mindfully, Anirvan suggests we imagine Brahman consciousness flowing from everywhere in the cosmos, and coiling down into the individual soul or Self as the lungs suck in air.

Then, on the out-breath, visualize the air flowing back into the atmosphere above and around us. He says this movement unites the three Realities: Brahman (God or the Supreme Being), Atman (the individual Self) and Jagat (the World).

Anirvan assures us that the centering effect of such exercises is not autosuggestion: "You have not created it. You have only discovered it." Gurdjieff has said that there are many finer elements in the air that nourish us only when we breathe in with conscious awareness.

Here is some of the science behind how attention to the breath brings us back into balance. Deep, relaxed breathing activates the *vagus nerve*—the longest nerve of the autonomic nervous system—which travels all the way from the brain to the digestive system. It originates in the brain as cranial nerve ten, travels down from the neck and then passes around the digestive system, liver, spleen, pancreas, heart and lungs.

It is a major player in the *rest-and-digest* part of us, sending signals back and forth between gut and brain. So if you suffer from digestive disturbances, high blood pressure, depression or any inflammatory condition, you might consider bringing your attention more often to your breath, in order to initiate a shift toward relaxation. It will also lead to better blood-sugar regulation and reduce the risk of stroke, cardiovascular disease and migraines.

The vagus nerve *reads* the gut *microbiome* and responds to any inflammation. It provides two-way communication, which means that that whatever is going on in your gut affects your mood, stress levels, and overall well-being. And the opposite is also true. Your stress levels and whatever you are thinking and feeling directly affect your gut. Without your being aware of it, all day long your *microbiome* is listening to your thoughts, attitudes, and emotions—and reacting to them.

Does what you are doing seem so important that you feel you have no time to breathe? Make note of the times when you hold your breath under stress. Bring your conscious attention to the fact. Live for a moment in the tension between the breath-holder in you and the one who wishes to let it go. That way you interfere for a moment with the power your fight-or-flight nervous system has over you.

The good news is that, when we allow the rhythm of our breath to slow down, we stimulate the vagus nerve and increase our *vagal tone*. The bigger the difference between breathing in, which speeds up the heart-rate, and breathing out, which slows it down, the better your vagal tone. You will feel happier, have less anxiety and more resilience in the face of stress.

To improve your vagal tone, let slow, rhythmic breathing take over from time to time in your day. Lying on your back for ten minutes on the floor is a great way to do it, because that also invites your spine to lengthen and your back to strengthen. Whenever you notice that you are taking shallow breaths from the top of the lungs, pause in your rush forward and allow the breathing to deepen and fill up more of your torso, including the belly.

Humming or singing will always be helpful because the vagus nerve is considered the 'parent' of the nerves that control the voice box. Sing your favorite songs as you work. Hum the sound *OM* in a low voice when you feel pressured, or encourage yourself by muttering positive sayings out loud.

Another way to improve vagal tone is to splash cold water on your face. I do it every morning to wake myself up. And it will come as no surprise that feelings of goodwill towards yourself and others also improve vagal tone. Finally, think about balancing your gut *microbiome* with a high-quality *probiotic*. Earth–based is good. The presence of healthy bacteria in the gut will create a positive feed-back loop through the vagus nerve, increasing its tone.

As your awareness fluctuates throughout the day, you will inevitably be pulled away from rootedness in yourself, whether to attend to the person with whom you are talking or the chair you are about to sit on. Engage often in the practice of interrupting your busyness with seven conscious breaths at certain moments in your day. Observe the flow of your breath in and out. Remind yourself that this is the breath of life, sourced from the core of consciousness.

Then, as your breath deepens and your busyness quiets down, listen to all the voices in yourself that are still competing for your attention. Gradually separate out the deeper call of the still small voice in the heart. Each time you tune in to the breathing you will discover where *you* really are, and what is taking you away from home base. To come closer to home base, move on to *Step Six: Aligning Body, Mind and Heart.*

Aligning Body, Mind and Heart

Staying in Front of the Lack
*"Sometimes I go about pitying myself while all the time I am
being carried on great wings across the sky."*
Ojibwa song

Do you sometimes wake up to how imperfect you are—not the way
you want to be? Maybe you felt jealous when you wanted to feel
loving, lashed out when you wished to be understanding, said the
wrong thing—and on and on. There are endless possibilities for
human frailty.

But what to do when you are shocked awake by a sense of failure?
One choice is to *bury yourself* in activity. Another is self-attack. In
either case, you are fleeing present reality, avoiding the truth of the
moment. Instead you could choose to stay there, in the often
extreme discomfort of seeing what is.

"Stay in front of the lack," urged Jeanne de Salzmann when we told
her we didn't like what we saw in ourselves. It is a powerful exercise, instantly available to those who seek greater self-awareness.
Stay in the discomfort of seeing what's going on rather than fleeing
the scene or improving on it. That is the work of *becoming present*
in a nutshell.

The pain you feel is like a fire that burns away what is unreal.
Instead of disapproving, ignoring, or criticizing yourself for how
you are, accept to bear the uncertainty, confusion, and mixed
messages that inevitably appear.

It's not easy. In fact, it's so uncomfortable to stay there that we
almost never try. But once again our Body Being can anchor our
effort. Turn your attention immediately to whatever physical position you find yourself in. Just as when you become aware of a slump,
you typically might want to pull your shoulders back in an attempt
to be *super-straight*, what if you decided to stay right there and
explore how slump or super-straight actually *feels*?

Sense the curving back as you slump over or get inside how the chest feels as you press it forward like a pigeon's to straighten up. In other words, let yourself *live* whatever position you find yourself in, mental, physical, or emotional.

Do the same with reactions of disapproval. Remain in the discomfort of not liking what you thought or did, in the midst of self-disgust, self-justification, or whatever is going on. Discover the sensations that are vibrating in every inch of your body. Acknowledge your dissatisfaction; feel the reaction that sets in.

As you continue to look into the mirror of your thought and action rather than turning away toward improvement, a gradual change in your state will take place. Then, if you can manage to stay a little longer witnessing the discomfort, not avoiding or *end-gaining* in the usual way, a release of mental, emotional, and physical tension will occur all by itself.

Take a living snapshot of yourself. Then gradually expand your attention to include more of who you are. Remind yourself of the three receptive centers through which you process life. What data is your heart gathering? What messages is your body/mind sending out into the world? Say hello to all your body parts while you check out what thoughts are a-thinking in you, and what emotions express themselves through you.

To stay in front of the sense that you have gone off balance is a high aim. It is similar to the effort of *Deep Practice* that professional athletes and other top performers employ to perfect their skills. Rather than attempting to better what's already pretty good by repeating it, they go to the area of most difficulty and work where they tend to stop, fall down on the job, or give up in despair. They accept that the work is slow, deliberate and awkward, and that it demands complete commitment from an active body and brain. But they know from first-hand experience that it works.

Here's why: deep practice builds *myelin*, a sheath which wraps around and insulates your nerve fiber chains to make your living circuitry faster and more accurate. It is behind the growth of both mental and physical skills. While it increases more rapidly in childhood, it is ours to develop all our life long.

Daniel Siegel says it is three thousand times faster in soccer players. For really high skill, you need ten thousand hours of practice—known as the Talent Lock. "Deep Practice is the opposite of going to what's already good and repeating it over and over to make it better," he explains. "The best athletes go to the area of deficit and work in the hard places!"

That is what we are doing any time we go against the habit of running away from our own truth. As we stay with the impression of how we have lost touch with ourselves, we approach the reality we are living through.

So every time you discover that your body is tied up in knots, your thoughts running amok, or your reactivity going full blast, stay there and make an effort at Deep Practice. As F. M. Alexander explained to his students, "When you stop doing the wrong thing, the right thing does itself."

Becoming Pervious
*"Love becomes possible when we see the other
with the eye of the heart."*
Marion Woodman

You may have spent many years as I did, trying to be as impervious as possible to the slings and arrows delivered by life. Childhood experiences lead many of us to build a defensive fortress against unexpected attacks. Then one day we wake up to the fact that we have walled ourselves in even as we worked to keep aggressors out. If that sounds like your situation, it may be time for you to become more pervious.

Why is this so important? Because you need to know more about the real forces behind the choices you make. When I began to scrutinize my own inner defense system, I discovered an inner Tyrant inside, running the show. For years I had thought he was the voice of my conscience, with my best interests at heart. But when I became suspicious of his negative attitude toward me and began to dialogue with him, I learned that this harsh, endlessly critical authority figure inside my head was neither my conscience nor my friend. He was an inner *persona* or *complex* that destroyed my confidence and often spoiled my relationships with others.

You, too, may have built up inner psychic armor to protect yourself from early fears and failures. In fact we have all created some kind of unconscious self-defense system to minimize the blows of life. And as Donald Kalsched makes clear in *The Inner World of Trauma*, "under the pressure of repeated disappointments and disillusionments . . . our inner protectors turn into persecutors." In other words, the protector we created to keep others out of our private inner world can turn against us with criticism and contempt, creating a split between the hypercritical ego and a part of ourselves that long ago fled into unconsciousness.

Today, as grownups, we inevitably retain some fragments of this persecutor. For example, with or without being aware of it, you may feel contempt for your own vulnerability and innocence. Investigate whether there is a totalitarian inner caretaker in you who sets up a wall of self-hate and hyper-criticism of others to save you from further suffering.

Kalsched insists that repair of this dissociated psychic part depends less on insight and more on experience in the body. Recovery of your innate sense of Self will take place gradually as you deepen your experience of Body Consciousness. You will become less fearful and more pervious to unknown aspects of yourself.

So if you haven't yet tried dialoguing, as suggested earlier, with those parts of you that criticize or boss you around, you might find it worthwhile. These inner personas or complexes limit our freedom and tie us down to the past as they motivate or punish us without our suspecting their power.

Only when we begin to differentiate them from the person we consciously believe ourselves to be can we awaken to the scope of their influence. Then we can separate from them, little by little, through Deep Practice.

If you want to study this further, ask your inner scientist to write down what you think you already know about yourself. What do you like, what do you not like, in yourself and others? Have you discovered persona fragments like my tyrant that take you over? If so, remind yourself that they don't reflect who you really are. They only indicate the way you deal with what you've been dealt by life. Dialogue with them to find out more about them.

One way to do this is to experiment with Jung's Active Imagination exercise. Choose a medium such as painting, sculpting, writing, dancing, musical composition, or any means of self-expression in which the controlling consciousness plays second fiddle to the world below the mind. Focus on a recently discovered persona, an overblown emotional reaction, or a disturbing dream image. Immerse yourself in Body Consciousness as you offer it a listening mind and hand so it can express itself through you.

Let the brush or words move freely on the paper or the clay form itself between your fingers. Or put on your favorite music and allow your body to go freely into movement. While it's important for the mind to stay present as a witness, don't let it dominate or correct what you are doing. Allow a perhaps unknown part of yourself to act while you watch.

You will discover that there's a lot you already suspect but almost never tune into. To find out more, ask any emotional habit, dream image, or inner persona to explain why it is there and what it thinks of you. If an accusation comes at you from inside, ask to have it explained. Tell the inner critic you want to understand why. Don't hesitate to ask these fragments of your personality for help.

It is also helpful to bring to consciousness some of the comments your mind makes about yourself or other people. Just where are they coming from? Give these personas a name—Judge, Tyrant, Terrorist, Pleaser, God's Little Helper, Little Friend of All the World—to begin to differentiate them from your own core of truth. They are not you. They are members of the cast of characters in your human drama, some helpful, some hateful, some useful. Get to know them.

While it's hard to listen to an unpleasant truth someone else tells you about yourself, it may be a lot harder to accept what your own personality fragments say about you—even when you may already suspect it's true. At the same time, try not to judge them or yourself.

When judgments inevitably appear, remind yourself that a scientist doesn't spend much time criticizing the results of his or her experiments. You are in your own private laboratory, discovering more about yourself as you become more pervious to who you are, to other people, and to new ideas and experiences.

Making a Conscious Shift

"Like light itself, (the soul) lives 'between the worlds'—now particle, now wave—always evanescent, just out of reach, leading us both out into the world and back into the depth of ourselves."
Donald Kalsched

We know how busy we are. We even sometimes suspect that our busyness can be a way of avoiding something. Or I could be *here* later, but right now I need to finish what I'm doing. As if *Doing* involves action and *Being* is about staying still. Body Consciousness can awaken you to the fact that Doing and Being are actually two sides of the same gold coin—yours to spend or hide away in a drawer under the scarves.

Nevertheless, to bring your Doing together with your Being needs a lot of attention. It is an effort against the habits of a lifetime. In order to bring them into closer relationship with each other, you will have to shift away from the ninety percent of waking hours most of us spend operating from the sympathetic nervous system— always ready for fight, flight or freeze.

Invest more of your time in the parasympathetic system, the rest-and-digest part of us that's not under our conscious control. It's the system responsible for breathing, heartbeat, and the digestive processes.

In *Views from the Real World*, Gurdjieff speaks about "the movements men call *work*." We don't usually think of our work in the world as simply another form of movement. In fact, when we say *work*, we often mean *drudgery*. But whatever you are doing is a movement of energy, *your* energy. It is an activity in which body and mind could come together creatively. When that happens, *Doing* and *Being* turn toward each other.

The choice is yours—to *bury yourself* in your activities or engage in what you are doing with all of your Being. To invest your energy and attention in Body Consciousness or remain immersed in habit. To attend to your Self along with whatever movements you make.

Here's one way to try: commit to a *Conscious Shift*. As we've seen in *Staying in Front of the Lack*, whenever I become aware of myself and don't like what I see, I automatically try to change my state to feel better. But the wish to change the present is a projection into the future, or a yearning for the past that has nothing to do with your life here and now.

So if your first thought is *"How to get more done?"* go deeper. Ask instead, *"How to be?"* You are consciously shifting your attention from whatever you are doing to include what you are feeling and sensing at this very moment.

"What's really going on here?" you might ask. Or "How do I *feel* about this?" Or even *"Who is here doing this?"* The answer may come in a sense of heaviness, of not being *tuned* to the present moment, Remind yourself that you aren't yet in a balanced, three-centered state.

As you continue to witness what's going on, the inner hubbub will become quieter. Your attention already began to shift as soon as you engaged in taking stock of how and who you are. Accept whatever you find consciously: "This is how it is/I am." Then ask, *"Who is seeing this?"*

Your thought, turned toward the sensation of yourself, creates a magnet. Feelings immediately appear. As you stay there, with your whole being in question, judging nothing, sensing everything, the different energies of mind and body, connected through the *axis of creation* in the spine, will begin to find each other.

A finer energy will appear as the head attends to the heaviness of the body, the heart attends to the distracted mind, and a tentative new sense of balance between them makes itself known.

Soon life, with its ordinary movements, will intervene. You discover that you alternate between seeking a path to spirit and identifying with the joys and sorrows of this life on earth. But what if *you are the path?* And, if so, where are you taking yourself?

Perhaps you, like me, sought a crowning achievement rather than accepting to be a work-in-progress. Life teaches us that food for Being is necessary every day and no one super-effort will get us to the top of Jacob's ladder.

Commit often to making a Conscious Shift. Then, as Body Consciousness awakens and awareness of the sensation of your existence deepens, you will experience the re-gathering of all the energy lost in complaint, annoyance, judgment, avidity, or any other reaction. Your attention will be drawn toward the powerful Presence that lives in you and calls on you to attend to it.

Cultivating the Three Treasures
"The first sign of obedience to something greater
is conscious sensation."
Jeanne de Salzmann

There are many approaches to developing body, mind, and heart. The Great Work of Hermes Trismegistus is one of the earliest—the search for the Philosopher's Stone. Buddhists work to train the mind in order to move beyond a life of suffering. Hindus look to connect with Buddhi, or higher mind—a witness who sees, knows, and discriminates. The Bhagavad Gita tells us that there is a field (creation), a knower of the field (you and me), and the one in each of us who knows both the field and its knower. Krishna, the all-seeing Consciousness, is the knower of the field in all fields.

Gurdjieff's approach differs in that he calls on us to work simultaneously on head, heart and body in what is referred to as The Fourth Way, or Work in Life. He explains that in the Way of the Fakir the body is unceasingly punished to strengthen the will, while the Monk shuts himself in a monastery to develop love through prayer and fasting; and the Yogi dedicates his life to work directly on mind-consciousness. But once each of them has fully developed their primary path, they must begin to work on the other two aspects of their Being.

The Fourth Way intends a work on all three paths at once while we function in ordinary life. The aim is to come under the influence of our two higher centers, which exist on another level of thought and feeling. Unfortunately for us, although they are fully operational and send us messages from time to time, our so-to-speak lower equipment isn't up to the task of receiving their higher vibrations. The Fourth Way works to prepare our planetary selves so that someday we will be able to come under the influence of Higher Mind and Higher Feeling.

Daoists also work on all three paths at once. The aim of Qigong, Tai Chi, and the other martial arts is to develop *intrinsic energy*— the energy of Being—by strengthening the body, concentrating the wandering mind, and tuning out the constant emotional reactivity that imprisons us.

They describe the Qi, Chi, or Divine Elixir as a creative energy that exists everywhere in the universe. In humans it is centered in three *dantians* or *elixir fields* located in the belly brain, the chest or *heart-mind,* and the head brain.

Specifically, the lower dantian is located a couple of inches below the navel, deep within the belly. The middle dantian is in the *heart-mind* or Crimson Palace, where vitality is refined into spirit. And the upper dantian rests behind the forehead at the height of the Wisdom Eye. They are the wellsprings of our *Three Treasures*— Wisdom, Love, and Vitality.

In Robert Peng's classes, videos and book, *The Master Key,* he teaches a series of psychophysical exercises to access, strengthen, and balance these three dantians with each other. You learn to take four full-body positions somewhat similar to *Stand like a Tree.* You are grounded, erect, knees slightly bent and with feet shoulder width apart, 'rooted' in the earth.

In the first position your arms circle diagonally upward with hands above the head, palms turned toward the sky, to receive Universal Chi. The space between arms and head is an open circle, as if you held up a beach ball. "Feel the essence of your Wisdom Qi flow inside the ball between your hands," says Peng.

In the next position, aimed at developing increased vitality, you form an open circle with your arms diagonally forward and down, fingers pointing toward each other, palms and thoughts turned toward the lower dantian to access the energy of earth. "Imagine that your feet are roots sinking deep into the ground as you absorb Earth Qi through your legs," Peng indicates.

In the third position, the open circle of your arms is at shoulder level, palms turned toward the chest, to invite a compassionate heart. "Imagine that you are hugging the horizon," says Peng. "Become aware of the Human Qi and your own Love Qi empowering your willpower, infusing it with compassion and tenderness."

Finally, there is a Universal Posture in which you focus on the vertical line that runs from the top of the head down to the earth at your feet called the Central Meridian. It connects all three dantians and helps to harmonize their energy.

In this position one arm is curled downward, palm turned up at the level of the lower dantian, while the other forms a vertical line in front of your upper chest, fingers pointed upward. Peng advises you to "Expand your Central Meridian both above your head up into the sky and down into the Earth below your feet. Feel the Three Treasures blending inside the central core of your body."

He tells us that when they work harmoniously, the upper dantian—source of intelligence and creativity—will provide the energy to make the right decisions. The lower dantian—center for vitality, health, strength and support—can act on the good ideas from above and bring them to fruition with the assistance of the middle dantian—a compassionate heart.

If you wish to cultivate the Three Treasures, start by staying in one of these positions for three to five minutes a day. Then, as you are able to stand a little longer, add one or more of the others. You want to get to the point where you can stay at least three minutes in each of them, and end poised in the vertical channel that unites them.

The first few minutes of standing can be uncomfortable. We aren't used to standing still and just being here. But if you root yourself in your feet and release any tense places in your body, as described earlier, your breathing will deepen and you will begin to feel an increased circulation of energy.

This exercise works to open up the stuck places in our body/mind and release the tension served up to us every day by the stress of modern life. The balance between the three centers takes precedence over strengthening one or another.

For example, to return to balance when you are in a highly emotional state, focus on the Wisdom Eye as you take the position that corresponds to it. Stay there for a while to let the brou-ha-ha in your heart quiet down.

Or if you've been wrapping your head around a problem for too long, and feel you've lost touch with your humanity or your flesh and bones, stand first in the heart position, or focus on increasing your vitality in the lower dantian. Then, when you feel the flow of new energy in response, move on to the next position.

Applying Four Keys to Well-Being
"It is not enough to be busy. So are the ants. The question is: What are we busy about?"
Henry David Thoreau

Are you ready to change the world by changing your response to it? According to Richard Davidson, a pioneer in contemplative neuroscience at the University of Wisconsin at Madison, our three main neural functions—*regulation, learning,* and *selection*—can be excited or inhibited by strengthening some circuits of the brain and weakening others. He insists that "the brain can be transformed through engagement with purely mental practices derived from the world's great religious traditions . . . the brain, more than any other organ in our body, is the organ built to change in response to experience."

Davidson, author of *Altered Traits: Science Reveals How Meditation Changes Your Mind, Brain, and Body,* has made MRIs of Tibetan monks in such meditative states as visualization, one-pointed concentration, and the generation of compassion. He offers neurological proof that "Well-being is a skill, fundamentally no different than learning to play the cello. If one practices the skills of well-being, one will get better at it." At the Greater Good Science Center's conference he recently explained how each of his four keys to well-being relates to activity in our neural circuits.

The first key is *Resilience*. How quickly can you recover from adversity? Because life happens in spite of all our plans, we can't protect ourselves from accident or fate. However, we *can* change the way we react to it. Davidson did a lot of research on whether specific brain circuits can be altered by regular practice in simple mindfulness meditation. Although the long-term answer is yes, it turns out that you need several thousand hours of practice before you can see real improvement in your resilience. (Nevertheless he advises us to keep meditating.)

He calls the second key *Outlook,* "the flip-side of resilience," and offers good news: the simple practices of loving kindness and compassion meditation may alter this circuitry quite quickly, after a modest dose of practice. What we need to develop here is the ability to recognize what's positive in others, to savor positive experiences, and to think of other human beings as innately good.

In one study people who had never before meditated were randomly assigned to one group and given a secular form of compassion training. The second group worked on cognitive reappraisal training, an emotion-regulation exercise that comes from cognitive therapy. In the compassion group, brain circuits were strengthened after only seven hours—30 minutes of practice a day for two weeks.

The third key is *Attention*, for which Davidson points to the Harvard study mentioned earlier, in which researchers asked people on their smart-phones, in the middle of their busy day, what they were focused on and how happy they felt at that moment. Since forty-seven percent of the time people weren't paying attention to what they were doing, Davidson wonders how that would impact productivity, or listening to and staying present to another person.

Number four is *Generosity*. Davidson says there's plenty of data to show that when people are generous and altruistic "they actually activate circuits in the brain that are key to fostering well-being. These circuits get activated in a way that is more enduring than the way we respond to other positive incentives, such as winning a game or earning a prize. He explains that "When we engage in practices that are designed to cultivate kindness and compassion, we're not actually creating something that didn't already exist. What we're doing is recognizing, strengthening, and nurturing a quality that was there from the outset."

Because our brains are constantly being shaped and reshaped by the way we live, we have the power to strengthen these four aspects of well-being. "In that way," concludes Davidson, "we can take responsibility for our own minds."

Standing in Your Own Truth
"You can't just sit down and talk about Truth. It doesn't work that way. You have to live it to understand it."
Rolling Thunder

We stray from reality whether we view life in terms of how things *ought* to be, or simply row our boat "gently down the stream." What's more, to seek inhuman perfection or think of life as "but a dream" is to miss out on the inner strength that comes from going against the automatic flow of life. So if you have turned your all-to-human craft around to struggle against the current, you are headed in the right direction.

Why make such an effort? Much of our morality and opinions are derived from the *collective*, gathered as we follow the crowd, and present ourselves to the world the way our parents, friends, or colleagues expect us to be. The danger, as Rilke pointed out, is that we grow up as masks.

Instead of giving in to outer demands so as to avoid rocking the boat, why not begin to peel off everything that's in the way of becoming your true Self—the person you were born to be? You and I have been given a lifetime to do just that, in the face of collective pressures that expect us to conform to society's choices.

Wise guides have even told us how to go about it. Many centuries ago, Hermes Trismegistus advised his students, "Don't be borne downstream. Make use of the back flow." And the *Secret of the Golden Flower* recommends *the backward-flowing method.*

In our time, one of the central practices of the Gurdjieff teaching is to work against the downward flow of *The Ray of Creation*, in which active energies devolve into the more passive, and life becomes more automatic. So if you wish to discover the real, unvarnished *you*, push your craft upstream toward the source—the Sun of all Suns.

To do this, start by investigating what you really want and like, rather than what you've appropriated as yours through imitation and the demands of authority figures. Pass all your attitudes and opinions through the sieve of your best intelligence. Write down in your notebook what you think is really *your own*, a result of your best thought, feeling and experience. That way you can meet up with who you are, and who you are not.

The work of separating what's yours and what isn't will give you courage to take the more difficult next step, which is to look into all that you have said a firm *no* to in the past. Throw light on those shadow parts that you put aside as you grew up because you or others disapproved of them. Uncover the unique being that you are.

In my case, it took a long time to realize that truth wasn't to be found in reading more books or doing more stuff. The heroic image of Jacob wrestling with the angel satisfied me for many years as I grappled with how *to become Myself*.

Finally I discovered that in spite of my deep longing for spiritual experience, any state of tension or blind determination moved me away from what I sought. *Doing battle* wasn't getting me anywhere, because what I desired above all else must be sought delicately, with the recognition that I don't really know how to get there from here.

I pass this on in the hope that it won't take others the lifetime it took me to discover that seeking an experience of the sacred is not a tensing of inner wish-muscles. Rather, it is a letting go of everything, including the neediness to know—a release from the desperation to find something more 'spiritual.'

When you let go, prepare to enter a no-man's-land beyond thinking, doing, and reacting. Beyond the hankering and dejection in which we live. To arrive at a place where you can stand in your naked truth, you must learn how to pause and listen at the threshold.

Then, if access is granted to that elusive space, you can listen and wait some more. Wait like a hunter—silent and unmoving, alert in every direction for the gift of life. Wait long enough so that knowing and loving can find you. We are not here to change ourselves but to learn how to bring ourselves under those influences that make change possible.

patience

Lucky for us, just as the body always seeks to heal itself, there are forces in our psychic world that move us toward becoming who we are. Someone sits quietly somewhere inside, bearing witness to all that goes on without judging. It may take days, months or years to digest what that witness has seen, but the truth of it will lead you home in yourself.

As you pull oars against the automatic flow of life, be alert to any tendency to trash yourself for not living up to elephant-sized expectations. Notice when you are closer to who you really are, when you are acting out a part, or dredging up answers to satisfy others or silence your own doubt.

Self-attack will always get in the way. Rather, when you feel the need to improve yourself, get down on the ground and make friends with your own human nature. Move the body, allow the breath to deepen, and clear the monkey mind. Over coffee, on a walk, or in meditation, open to the mystery of who you are.

Settling Down on Rumi's Field
"You are not a drop in the ocean, you are the entire
ocean in a drop."
Rumi

Perhaps Rumi said it best: "Out beyond ideas of wrong-doing and right doing, there is a field. I'll meet you there." We all need to find that field beyond guilt and responsibility, beyond sin and redemption, where there's rest for the busy mind, always arguing, elaborating, affirming, condemning, criticizing. Rest for the anguished heart as it seeks meaning in a confusing world, full of conflicting demands. And rest from the insidious fear that we'll be caught out because, in spite of all our good intentions, we're sure to get it wrong again.

One path to Rumi's field includes listening intently to the spaces between the many words we hear and speak. Another is attending to the sound of silence itself. The space between our achievings is non-invasive. It doesn't demand action, but provides nourishment. You could call it *Endless Time,* where you feel cared for, liberated from the sense that you must perform, get stuff done, realize a potential, serve a cause, help a friend.

The fact is, it is always here—ready to flood in whenever you can give up for a moment the problems that seem so immediate, so real. A world of sound, touch, taste, smell, and unrecognized feelings could be the place where joy begins.

While Endless Time can seem like prayer or meditation, casting off the cares of the day for a private moment of quiet in the back room, the strange thing is that this wider space can open just as easily on a crowded subway platform where a mass of humanity hurries to their next thing. Exchange a sympathetic look with a fellow passenger and you immediately feel connected to all these rushing lives, as full of joy and fear and investments in relationships as yours. Then the noise recedes and inner quiet floods in from a world beyond time.

It was on such a subway platform that I woke up to what was left of my life. Standing there, waiting for the next train and immersed in the usual inner complaints, suddenly I heard a song belted out by a black woman with a voice like an organ. *"YESTERDAY'S GONE,"* she sang, her voice resonating throughout the tunnel. Then, more quietly and sadly she added, *"Tomorrow may never be mine."*

The truth of her words hit me like a bolt of lightning. Yes, yesterday provided me with lots of striving and satisfying of desires. And the thought of tomorrow gets me up in the morning to go to work. But what about today, all by itself? Suddenly I was lost. I felt undone, exposed, unreal. And then she sang:

"Lord for my sake
Teach me to take
One day at a time."

There it was. "Sufficient unto the day." And sometimes I couldn't even handle a day! I went toward the singer, grasping a ten-dollar bill as an inadequate thank you. We faced off, looked into each other's eyes and embraced as my tears came. Friends for life who would probably never see each other again. But intimately knowing and being known.

Do you carry a lot of yesterday around with you? Notice how often you call up past memories, or relive moments you lived through only an hour or two before. Listen to how you talk to yourself, and how often you tell yourself, " If only I had said or done this or that;" or "I wish something different had happened, then all would be well."

Take note of what you accuse yourself of. We often attack ourselves for being unsatisfactory. But who's the judge of that? Did you try your best? Maybe yes, maybe no. Either way, accept it as a fact. Remind yourself again that you aren't unsatisfactory. You are unfinished.

An old soldier shared with Gurdjieff his life-changing experience on the front lines in World War I. He had tried to save a wounded buddy by carrying him on his back. But when they arrived at the medic's tent he saw that his friend's body had covered him like a shield. It was riddled with bullets aimed at both of them. How to get rid of a lifetime of guilt that his buddy had died protecting him? *"Accept it like your skin,"* advised Gurdjieff.

You may not have hauled a bullet-ridden body on your back, but we all carry guilt and suffering from what we have done or left undone—sometimes too difficult to bear. Nevertheless, to move on into your present life, you need to accept it as an aspect of the unique, wounded, imperfect human being that you are; that we all are.

Maybe you are able to lay the past to rest, but spend too much time and energy worrying about what might happen in the future. If so, try this for a week. Whenever you become aware of such a state, make a note of when and why it appeared. In the evening, read over what you wrote about during the day.

Was the energy you spent on that particular anxiety worth the candle? If not, see if you can blow that particular candle out by recognizing it for what it is—escape from your present life.

Finally, as you become aware of how often you spend time with your thoughts on either the past or the future, set your findings down in two columns. Which is longer, past or future? Wonder to yourself why this is so. Does where you have been focused feed the soul?

No matter whether past or future calls you more frequently, the fact is that today is all we have. Tomorrow may never be ours. Now is the only reality. How to move into our present life? Let's turn to Step Seven: *Forging New Relationships with Yourself and Others.*

Forging New Relationships with Yourself and Others

Living the Questions
"The response to your question comes from above and below.
You are yourself the answer."
Talking with Angels

We are never rewarded for being confused or uncertain. We are expected to state our opinions firmly as befits citizens of a free society, brought up to honor answers more than questions. Problem is, we often repeat what we've heard from others as if it were true.

And don't we mostly depend on the head-brain alone for the answers? As psychiatrist Michel de Salzmann points out in his essay on *Man's Ever New and Eternal Challenge*, "When born in the mind, the question calls forth an answer through the mind and keeps me divided under my compulsion for explanation and for power over my object world. Understanding needs more. It needs experiencing."

How to ground the questing mind in the experiences of daily living? You already know the answer by now. Develop Body Consciousness! In fact, when we listen to the inner questions that arise from our experience, life becomes a spiritual path. When we stop listening, we have lost our way.

Sooner or later we waken with a painful pang, a sense of loss, a surge of dissatisfaction in how we are/life is. According to Rumi, this dissatisfaction is lawful and inevitable. He says we weren't born to live content: "There is in man a passion, an agony, an itch, an importunity such that though a hundred thousand worlds were his to own, yet he would not rest nor find repose. These creatures dabble successively in every trade and craft and office; they study astronomy and medicine and the rest, and take no repose; for they have not attained the object of their quest."

If dissatisfaction with our lives is wired into us as human beings, we can either recognize the importance of honoring questions—along with the discomfort of not knowing the answer—or run from them as Orestes did, pursued by the Furies.

After a lifetime of suffering, he finally turned toward them and listened. That's when they were transformed into the Eumenides. Perhaps inner peace can only be ours if we learn to love and live with our questions, rather than trying to silence them with answers.

History testifies to those who have wandered the world in dissatisfaction: the madman with the burning eyes and tortured soul who refuses to sleep in the same bed twice; the restless nomad of any religion—the Baul; the Sufi; or the Pilgrim who walks the world for decades repeating the Jesus prayer. If such seekers are lucky, they may find serenity in the deep acceptance of not knowing—as they *live* the division of body, mind and heart.

Brother Lawrence, the 16th century lay monk who never made it into the monastery's inner circle, followed a different path. *The Practice of the Presence of God* tells us how he gave himself up along with his questions, offering every movement of his body to God, whether sweeping the refectory floor or scrubbing out the great cooking pots.

Contemporary Hindu teacher Jean Klein suggests that since we can never know what we are, we need to learn more about what we are not. In *Ease of Being* he explains that dissatisfaction will kindle an "intimation of reality" which awakens a sense of lack. There may be a moment of peace when we get what we thought we wanted, but soon we will be off and running once more, "like a hunting dog who cannot find the scent."

As we gradually become more attracted to what Klein calls "the scent of reality," we can reassess our values and reorient ourselves toward our own true North. Gurdjieff says we need to develop a "magnetic center" that can guide us toward a place deep within that resonates with the sound of truth.

Reasoning minds may find it hard to accept that questions could be more important than answers, but poets and Zen masters know it to be true. Rainer Maria Rilke advised his young friend to be patient and live and love his questions rather than try to solve them. Zen masters assign *koans* that their disciples will pursue for days, months or even years, in search of a place beyond the thinking mind where the incomprehensible comes to rest in illumination. In order to arrive at such a place we must eat our questions with our breakfast and carry them with us like treasures through the day.

As you move through your duties today, challenge yourself with whatever question burns in your heart. Or if none comes to mind, you could ask yourself: "Am I wholly engaged?" Or "Is my action beneficial or detrimental to the rest of the world?"

You might interrupt yourself in the midst of your activities, with "What does the mind serve right now?" Jungian analyst James Hollis likes to ask his students, "What wants to come into the world through you?" Or "Have you stepped into your journey yet?"

Such questions may evoke grief or fear. Doubts and disbeliefs overwhelm us, thinking becomes foggy, vulnerability is suddenly front and center, and balance becomes more erratic. We know what to do and don't do it, and thus seem to be our own enemy. Our acquired sense of self gets in our way because it is in the service of how we interpret life—through our history, our patterns, and our various strategies to avoid conflict—rather than in the best interest of becoming who we really are.

Yet if we could absorb into our flesh and bones the various unsettling queries life throws at us, perhaps the unquiet spirit in us would find rest. As Jeanne de Salzmann says: "My existence itself is a question to which I am obliged to respond. My response is in the way I exist at the very moment . . . The challenge in the question is always new. It is the response that is old."

Discovering that "We Is What Me Is"

*"When we are present to ourselves we are present to others in a
totally new way . . . There is no egoism involved here, no need
to win or lose, no need to control. The projections have been
withdrawn and reclaimed as parts of ourselves. Only when
this happens is genuine relationship possible."*
Marion Woodman

According to Daniel Siegel, we are both an 'I' and part of an 'us.'
He points to the recently discovered *mirror neurons* that help
connect us to one another. They are like a hardwired system
through which we can intuit the mind-state of other people and
empathize with them. When someone communicates with you,
these neurons dissolve the border between you.

"Mirror neurons use right hemisphere signals to simulate the other
within ourselves and to construct a neural map of our interdependent sense of a 'self,'" Siegel explains. "It's the mid-prefrontal cortex
fibers that map out the internal states of others, and they do this not
only within one brain, mine, but also between two brains, mine and
yours, and even among many brains."

He says the brain is *exquisitely social*, and insists that emotions are
its fundamental language. "Through them we become integrated
and develop an emergent resonance with the internal state of the
other."

Siegel defines the *brain* as part of an embodied nervous system, a
physical mechanism through which both energy and information
flow to influence relationship and the mind. By *relationship* he
means the flow of energy and information between people.

As for *mind*, which both monitors and modifies what's happening,
it is "an embodied and relational process that regulates the flow of
energy and information, consciousness included." Mind isn't something each of us owns. Rather, it is shared between people. "We are
profoundly interconnected," he affirms. "We need to make maps
of *we* because *we* is what *me* is!"

So if you want to change your life and your relationships, study how
the brain receives input from the senses and gives it meaning.

According to Siegel, that's how blind people take in information and make an inner map of their world. The fact that they do this on secondary pathways rather than the main highways of the brain is a major clue to how we can bring about change.

"You can take an adult brain in whatever state it's in and change a person's life by creating new pathways," he insists. "Since the cortex is extremely adaptable and many parts of the brain are plastic, we can unmask dormant pathways we don't much use and develop them.

"A neural stem cell is only a blob, an undifferentiated cell in the brain that divides into two every twenty-four hours. But in eight to ten weeks, it will become established as a specialized neural cell and exist as a part of an interconnected network."

Neural firing leads to a mental experience and vice versa. When you think of your grandmother you have an immediate visual experience because the word triggers an electrical current running through the acoustic nerve fibers. It sends a message to the left hemisphere, where it is decoded and a visual image appears in other parts of the brain.

As your mind links past, present, and anticipation of the future, your experience of your grandmother creates a *neural net profile*. "No one on the planet knows how a neural firing turns into a mental image," says Siegel, "but we know where it happens and that it somehow leads to a subjective mental process. The mind emerges at the interface of neurobiology and the interpersonal transactions of experience between minds."

If you wish to build new neural pathways that can reshape your brain, relationship is the key element. "When we work with relationship, we work with brain structure," Siegel explains. "People rarely mention relationship in brain studies, but it provides vital input to the brain. Every form of psychotherapy that works, works because it creates healthier brain function and structure."

Integration is both the aim and the path forward—the vital connection with all our parts that leads to what we call Presence. Integration is what this book and its exercises are all about. At this very moment, through the practice of Body Consciousness, your integrative fibers are growing. You learn to be more open to others and more authentic within yourself. This will bring you a sense of deeper well-being as you develop more compassion for yourself and others.

According to Siegel, integration is made up of both *differentiation* and *linkage*, and if either of them is lacking we are in trouble: "Relationships, mind and brain aren't different domains of reality," he explains. "The emergent process we call 'mind' is located both in the nervous system and in our relationships. So each time we tune into each other we grow integrative fibers in our brain."

If we can develop kindness, compassion, and resilience—a natural result of integration—these integrative fibers will help our embodied brain to be at its best. Coherence and well-being will be available to us, as well as a feeling of connection to a larger world.

However, it's not easy to shift the focus of our adult brains toward loving kindness to others. For one thing, our earlier interpersonal experiences may have created habitual unfriendly or suspicious attitudes. The nervous system fires up, the brainstem signals the need for fight or flight and we're unable to open ourselves to another person.

On the other hand, when we make a Conscious Shift in our attitude toward others, we activate a different branch of the brainstem that sends messages to relax the muscles of the face and vocal chords, as well as normalize both blood pressure and heart rate. So give your neighbor the benefit of the doubt. It will inevitably reverberate in you. Good health and receptivity to others go hand in hand.

Dancing with the Divine
"I'll dance with you if you'll dance with me,
"For I am the Lord of the Dance, said he."
Sidney Carter

Every *body* longs to move to express the feelings that rise from its depths. And whenever there is a need to express deep, non-verbal emotion, sacred movement begins. That is how humans have always acknowledged the rising of the sun, prayed for help, propitiated or thanked the gods, warded off evil, or cried out with joy. Even the simplest daily tasks like planting, harvesting, or weaving have been performed ritually with communal songs and gestures since ancient times.

Ritual movement offers a bridge from our ordinary, day-to-day existence to a deeper experience of life. Greek plays and medieval dramas invite a communal experience of what it means to be human; Christians share the body and blood of Christ; the Japanese focus their finest attention on the act of making tea. And the Mesoamerican god, Quetzalcoatl, dives down into hellish darkness every night in order to rise again as the morning star—a dramatic reenactment of our possibility of dying to yesterday in order to begin each day anew.

Such rituals are a call of body to soul and soul to body in search of a conscious union between them. Jewish mystic Adin Steinsaltz explains in *The Thirteen Petalled Rose* how the exchange works in both directions: "Just as the union of body and soul gives life to the body, so does it wrap the soul in material substance, providing it with the powers of the physical body."

What makes a movement sacred? Any act that includes the body even as it centers the mind can carry that special quality of soul if it is performed with humility and attention. That is why Steinsaltz deplores any separation of body from soul. He says "The principal action of the soul . . . lies not in its . . . remoteness from the physical world, but precisely in the world of living creatures. In its contact with matter . . . especially relations with its own body—the soul is able to reach far higher levels than it can in its abstract state of separate essence."

My lifelong experience of dance has been first and foremost with the sacred dances G.I. Gurdjieff brought back from isolated monasteries in Asia. These dances and movement exercises are a master class in Body Consciousness. They awaken us to our habitual patterns of thinking, feeling and moving.

By taking unaccustomed positions in unusual and sometimes conflicting rhythms we are called to engage all three of our centers at once. A deeper level of conscious attention appears. According to Gurdjieff, only new postures and unaccustomed rhythms can shake us out of our fixed repertory of intellectual and emotional attitudes, and awaken us to new impressions of who we are.

The practice of calling body, mind and heart together through movement is also central to Marion Woodman's pioneering work in *BodySoul Rhythms*. In her workshops and intensives we spent mornings discussing psychology, participants' dreams, and the current world crisis. Afternoons were dedicated to bodywork in a large empty room.

We began by lying relaxed on the floor and listening to the sound of our own voices from deep within. Then we went on to make slow exploratory movements from the core of ourselves, sometimes inviting dream images to lead the body into movement.

Later we would dance singly or work in pairs, and perhaps finish the afternoon with the Dance of Three (described below). In the evenings, we might make *papier-mache* masks with our own faces as models. At the end of the week, before we returned to a life that seemed for the moment very far away, Marion would ask what we were prepared to give up of our old life in order to honor what we had received and make it our own. Sacrifice is necessary, because the hardest part of real change is "to take the treasure home."

Authentic Movement, which owes its beginnings to Mary Whitehouse, also attempts to bring body and soul into consciousness. The principle is to sensitize and ground the body in order to express a more authentic movement of oneself. At its best it leads to openness, deeper listening, and a new level of self-trust. "The movement becomes 'authentic' when one is able to allow intuitive impulses to freely express themselves without intellectual directive," explains RN Germaine Frazer, who has been practicing it for thirty years. "The core of the movement experience is the sensation of moving and being moved at the same time."

Both *BodySoul Rhythms* and *Authentic Movement* can offer you the experience of moving freely in space. In Marion's intensives we often danced with our eyes closed while a partner both witnessed and protected us from bumping into another pair. In the Dance of Three, one of us would dance, another would protect, and a third would witness both. "The witness contains the experience without judgmènt, projection or interpretation," says Frazer. "Everyone should have that incredible experience of being held, seen, and witnessed by others."

You can put on music and practice holding this dual space with a friend, or try it alone as both dancer and witness. Begin from a quiet, meditative inner space, perhaps with an important question at the back of your mind, or an image that means something special to you.

Let the question or image lead the body into movement without telling yourself what to do. Although no one is there to watch, you are your own conscious witness. And as Tai Chi master T. T. Liang told me, there is always an *enemy* present in any ritual, even when you practice alone. Sometimes it manifests as a simple lack of attention. Learn to be present to your energy in movement.

Awakening to the Conscious Feminine
You fill up my senses
Like a night in a forest
Like the mountains in springtime
Like a walk in the rain . . .
John Denver

In spite of the tension that often flares up between the sexes, masculine and feminine energies are not in opposition. Like yin and yang, night and day, dark and light, they complement each other. However, many people experience them as opposites.

Some may have been brought up by domineering fathers or mothers who cracked the family whip—or, on the contrary, acted like milquetoast to their partners. Perhaps as adults we fell for, or were rejected by, the seductive damsel or ice-queen, the brilliant but untouchable Phd, or the handsome football hero type.

Or married a heavy-handed or absent husband; a paper doll or hardworking mother-wife with no time for dalliance. What's more, many have worked under demanding, unfeeling bosses of either sex who worshiped at the bottom line.

Personally, as the family wage earner for some thirty years, I grasped for success in what was mostly a man's world. I donned pants both literally and figuratively, and seldom wore a dress or thought about my feminine nature. When I heard Marion Woodman speak about the Conscious Feminine I asked what she meant. She explained that it's not about gender but about the feminine principle—alive but often suppressed in both men and women.

"The feminine is presence, and relatedness, and a heart that can open so that when you meet another person you actually see that person's authentic self," she declared. "The creative masculine is the surrendered imagination. My conscious feminine container surrenders to that creative masculine. Then life is intercourse with the Divine. Out of that union comes the Divine Child, the new consciousness."

Men and women contain both genders but few understand the importance of the Conscious Feminine. What is needed on both sides of the perceived divide is an effort to bring our skewed attitudes into awareness. When the feminine is brought to consciousness, the masculine responds with new authority. Equally, in the presence of the Conscious Masculine the dormant feminine awakens—Shakti responding to Shiva's call.

When I interviewed Marion for an article in *Parabola,* she explained that the Conscious Feminine is a state of being, of receiving other people, of holding paradox. While the patriarchal attitude, so dominant today, holds onto either/or attitudes, the feminine lives in a world of both/and. "The feminine enjoys the process," she said. "She is not glued on the product, but moves with presence so there's never a great gaping hole between you and other people.

"That *beingness* is in both men and women. All of us need the masculine, not the patriarchy but the masculine discrimination, discernment, capacity for clarity, and the courage to use a sword when necessary. Some things have to be cut out of our lives and courage and strength is involved in that masculine energy. It would be wonderful to bring those two together in one person, where you have the being, honoring whatever is happening, as well as the discernment."

As we sat facing each other she gestured toward me and added, "For me the space between us, between any two people, holds molecules that carry our presence. Matter is as conscious as spirit, but most of us fail to inhabit our bodies and consequently fail to project that presence.

"Not present where we are, we're either behind or ahead of ourselves, not seeing, hearing, smelling. And most of us are grappling with unconscious negative feelings, so there's animosity where there could be *numinosity*—the glory of knowing we are loved, as that positive energy pours into us from the other person."

A conscious relationship between a man and a woman is, of course, an ideal. Yet Marion makes it sound possible, like something you or I could be open to the very next time we meet a member of the opposite sex. "If I take time to breathe and look at you, and feel my body relax, my energy flows towards you," she explained. "But if I hold back or let negative feelings build up, you will be cut off or react angrily, even if they aren't expressed.

"The unconscious projects without our consciousness even knowing about it, so what's going on in my unconscious is going to reach into your unconscious and influence what happens between us. In an argument, a negative charge can go from the personal unconscious, which carries 10 volts, to the collective unconscious, which carries 100,000 volts!"

Body Consciousness is indispensable in the search for the Conscious Feminine because physical movement awakens energies that are dormant or even imprisoned in many parts of our nature. As Marion further explains in *Conscious Femininity*, "To feminine consciousness, the spiritual and the physical are two aspects of one totality. Spirit confirms body, articulates body's wisdom . . . 'As above so below' translates into 'as in the head, so in the belly;' the two are simultaneously present."

If our bodies are sacred vessels, the energy of the Conscious Feminine is divine. This goddess energy can take many forms, from Shakti to the Black Madonna, to the girl-child who lives down the block. Authoritative, forthright and unsentimental, *She* demands that we work for Her embodiment in us.

117

In Marion's work, soul is the connecting link between the body and the divine. She calls psychological work *soul work*—soul being the eternal part of us that lives in the body for a few years. "Whenever the ego surrenders to the archetypal images of the unconscious, time meets the timeless," she explains. "Insofar as those moments are conscious, they are psychological, they belong to the soul . . . For me, soul-making is allowing the eternal essence to enter and experience the outer world through all the orifices of the body . . . so that the soul grows during its time on Earth. It grows like an embryo in the womb. Soul-making is constantly confronting the paradox that an eternal being is dwelling in a temporal body. That's why it suffers, and learns by heart."

Activating a New Feeling
"Each tiny cell prays,
And the prayer of all cells together is true feeling."
Talking with Angels

Each of us is born with an inner emotive furnace of creative energy that gradually dissipates over a lifetime. Artists tap into it, but many of us live unaware of how much power is contained within. Nevertheless, we more or less regulate our energy by releasing it in small or large reactions, and sometimes blow off huge quantities of steam.

Candace Pert offers a biological view of our situation in *Why You Feel The Way You Feel*: "When the biochemicals that are the substrate of emotion are flowing freely, all systems are united and made whole. When emotions are blocked, repressed, denied, not allowed to be whatever they may be, our network pathways get blocked, stopping the flow of the vital feel-good, unifying chemicals that run both our biology and our behavior."

Those who are afraid of their emotions often try too hard to control or repress them, whether through fear of hurting themselves or because they are afraid their anger might erupt all over their world. So they tamp down energy that can, over time, become an underground volcano. At that point a burst of anger can spew up so much 'lava' inside that they either implode or explode.

In order to have some control over your emotions, you need to understand deep in your bones that this is your own life force, your own energy, running away with you. As Body Consciousness develops, you will become more aware of the danger of unconsciously spewing your negative vibes to wound others and poison the world.

The first step is to become more aware of the sensation of your energy building up into an explosive reaction. Learn to distinguish the taste of self-pity or rage or other large emotions in their early stages. Remind yourself that this force can drive you where you don't want to go. Then, if you want to avoid a meltdown, try to refocus these negative feelings before they reach full blast.

Here's how it works: at the earliest moment you become aware of a negative feeling growing inside, consciously *change the direction of your attention*. Turn away from self-pity, complaint, criticism, outrage, or whatever is building up a head of steam. Instead, focus directly on the *physical sensations* of the forces at play in you.

It's important to make this effort as soon as a strong emotion begins to invade you, because once it is in full flood, you will have no control over it. Shift your attention right away to what's going on in your Body Being. Even say out loud, "this emotion is roiling my stomach," or "that thought makes my neck muscles stiffen," or "Feeling this way isn't worth it if it's going to give me back pain that lasts for days!"

Such efforts are at the very heart of change. When you show respect for your Body Being and acknowledge its autonomous existence, you are activating the possibility of help from another direction. Appreciate the cooperation that can be yours when you honor this intimate partnership.

Another way to begin the direct study of your emotions is to discover what *feeling tone* occupies your inner world most of the time. Although we are usually unaware of it, it is habitual—a part of who we have become. Other people often recognize it by the way we hold ourselves, or the timbre of our voice.

Are you often swayed by an undercurrent of anger—resenting what's happening to you? Or a wellspring of self-pity that brings you to feel victimized by life? Or do you maintain a falsely positive, good-girl attitude as I sometimes do, expressing a need to feel on top of my game, helpful to others, or cheerful in the face of difficulties? Once we recognize and begin to own our emotional tone, we will have a different relationship with it. It is not *me*, or *you*.

Like most of us, you probably also live in a state of diffuse anxiety. Inquire within whether you feel there is some other way you *ought to be*. As a child I often couldn't understand what adults and other children wanted from me. I lived in an alien world, trying to please others but mostly feeling unable to do so.

Body Consciousness is once again our best friend here, because there's a mathematical ratio between our level of anxiety, anger or pseudo-cheerfulness and our lack of kinesthetic awareness. The more grounded we are in our Body Being, the less we are invaded by anxiety and tension.

At the root of anxiety is the fear of death. James Hollis calls it "the single biggest neurosis of our time." He invites us to play the game of life with integrity, because "the quality of our life is the quality of our journey through it."

Let's take a leap into what might be called mysticism, now that leading-edge physics and neuroscience are proving that what we can't see or understand with our head brain is as real as an apple on a tree. Suppose for a moment that we are connected in some invisible way to every living being. That means our balance and vitality both depend on and assist all that's alive, including our very planet.

Our thoughts, our love, affect everyone and everything; and our wisdom mind is in contact with every living thing. In other words, as Rolling Thunder has assured us, we are all cells of Mother Earth.

Healing in the Quantum Field

"Where shall I look to praise you—upwards or downwards?
For you are space in which all things are contained.
There is no place but you."
Hermes Trismegistus

Perhaps it's time to embrace the fact that we live in a *quantum field*. Doug Bennett, author of *Life And Spirit In The Quantum Field*, calls it the ground of all being. "Everything that happens, happens in the quantum field," he explains. "Information in the quantum field is non-local and non-temporal—an active, creative intelligence at multiple levels. Human behavior and human health are quantum events and they are distributed across space (and time) in the field. This is what allows healing to take place across large distances."

According to quantum mechanics, *reality* is the quantum field, and what we see is a projection of the information contained in it. When early quantum-mechanics scientists discovered this, they began to take a closer look at Daoism, because Daoists and Buddhists say that material reality is an illusion and the real world is the spiritual world. From that perspective we are invited to consider the possibility that we are not a body containing spirit, but a body that lives in the embrace of spirit.

Biologist Rupert Sheldrake details his theory of *morphic fields* on his website, where he postulates that members of any social group are connected by a morphic field, even when they are many miles apart. Telepathy or ESP isn't abnormal or supernatural, he insists. It is even common between people who know each other well.

He then points out that mental activity is not confined to the insides of our heads. Rather, "mental fields extend far beyond our brain through intention and attention." In the same way that your cell phone reaches far beyond you to communicate with others, or the gravitational fields of the earth control the moon's orbit, the influence of mental fields spreads far beyond the physical reality of the brain.

We now know how particular frequencies and wavelengths of energy send signals that can affect the body in a positive, balancing way, producing interactions from molecule to molecule. And, as

121

science has only recently discovered, molecules don't have to touch each other to interact.

Healers all over the world practice their art with great respect for that spiritual component, as do acupuncturists, teachers of the Alexander Technique and the Feldenkrais Method, Reiki practitioners, Polarity and Craniosacral therapists, and those who practice Healing Touch and Therapeutic Touch. They develop a sensitivity that allows them to determine the energy flow in a client's body and detect where the blockages are.

Therapeutic Touch or Healing Touch is now taught in many nursing schools and hospitals, and practiced by some ten percent of the more than three million registered nurses in the U.S. As RN Ruth Rosenberg describes it, "The practitioner must *center*—becoming aware of and connecting with the presence of his/her own energy field, the client's energy field and also the universal energy field."

This centering is a result of deliberate intention and thinking, and has results similar to a meditative state. Many nurses not only acknowledge the relationship of *everything* (physical, mental, biochemical, emotional, environmental, etc), but also care for their patients with an awareness of these dimensions, which creates a healing environment in the mutually shared energy fields of self, patient, and universe. Rosenberg says that while its effects are mostly undocumented, nurses, patients and doctors have often witnessed and experienced them.

One new healing technique I experienced myself a few years ago after minor surgery is Electro Pressure Regeneration Therapy. I moistened two foam wraps and velcroed them around my ankles. A wire was clipped to each of them, leading out of a small box. It delivers a waveform that moves electrons through the body at a very low frequency, compatible to the naturally occurring electrical currents of the human body. Each time I plugged myself in (at least two hours at a time is recommended), the pain would quiet down within half an hour, my general state would improve, and I would fall gratefully asleep.

The manufacturers claim that these frequency ranges are optimal for clearing and enhancing the energy systems within the body via the internal energy meridian pathways—the same energy network used by Chinese physicians. Chinese medicine works with our body's energy flow over twelve meridians or channels that are normally well balanced.

But when this flow becomes blocked or weakened through injury, stress, fatigue or aging, the disruption can send the entire system off balance. Acupuncture, acupressure, tai chi, and qigong are all attempts to restore balance to the body's energy meridians by removing blockages from these channels.

Another new way of dealing with pain is cold laser therapy, also called low-level laser therapy or LLLT. While it has only become popular in the United States within the last twenty years, it has been used throughout the world since the 1960s. Simply put, it is a pain-less procedure that applies controlled light over sites of pain and injury to stimulate healing.

Lasers can replace over-the-counter medications in a variety of conditions ranging from headaches and low back pain to insomnia. Professional and high-level amateur athletes now use it, as do burn treatment centers, chiropractors, physical therapists and dentists. Oncologists have discovered that lasers can help reduce some of the severe symptoms of radiation and chemotherapy.

As more of the mystery behind healing is unveiled, we discover a two-way street in which the inner states of healer and patient converge under the benevolent influence of a mysterious third element. You can call it God, Creator, Universal Chi or the Quantum Field.

The fact is that therapists, shamans, and all energy healers are simply mediums between the sufferer and this flow of healing energy. Their job is to get their own stuff out of the way. Many a healer will respond to your heartfelt thanks at the relief you feel as does Steven Weiss, who simply nods acknowledgement and adds, "I just work here." As they all know, real healing comes from another level, and the more we learn to listen to our own body/mind, the deeper the healing we experience. Much is given. Sometimes we simply need to learn how to receive.

Spontaneous Combustion
*"No one can build you the bridge on which you, and only you,
must cross the river of life."*
Nietzsche

My way may not be your way. My dream is certainly not your dream. Each of us must wrestle with our own angels and demons as they drive us on to self-discovery. Yet we are not alone. I like to visualize the many paths that have spiraled up the sides of Mount Analogue since time began. While its summit is invisible, its base is accessible to all who seriously seek the meaning of their lives. We listen to their stories across the centuries, and as our paths merge from time to time, we brothers and sisters under a common sky encourage and support each other.

Which path is best for you? The mind's passionate pursuit of a larger understanding can call the body to vibrant life, just as the body can lead the distractible mind to a sacred space. And when they unite a deeper level of feeling is awakened.

So will you choose meditation in stillness to lead your thought toward the embrace of your Body Being? Zen masters see it as a royal road to illumination. Or would you perhaps do better to work at awakening Body Consciousness through some form of mindful movement?

Tai Chi and Qigong masters urge us to move with attention and intention. Legendary master Yang Cheng-Fu advises us to "Use your spirit and not your strength. Link the top to the bottom. Unify the inside to the outside. Move in the continuity—without interruption."

Attention is the key to every effort—attention to what you think, feel and do. As you engage in the world's work, consider a commitment that can bring all three of your receiving and transmitting systems into a balanced relationship with each other. Call on the prefrontal cortex in an effort at mindfulness. Sacrifice negative thoughts and reactions to regulate the limbic system (not so easy). And work to enliven your Body Being by calming the sympathetic nervous system through dedicated movement (an easier path for many people).

Whichever door you choose to open to these three rooms of your inner mansion, you will discover that a harmonious relationship between the head brain and the Body Being is essential. And whether you cultivate your attention in stillness or in action, the secret ingredient is release of tension. Let go of the old ways of holding onto yourself. Allow the river of your energy to run.

The challenge always begins as you return to daily activities. The golden thread of your attention seems to be sucked out of your Body Being and into everything you are looking at or thinking about. You wonder where your living Presence has gone, which Gurdjieff identifies as "the medium between personality and essence."

Each time you wake up to its loss, avoid self-pity or self-castigation. Simply go to work right away on the return. It can help to envisage that deeper connection as a moment of breathing in, and your distracted state as a moment of breathing out.

As the universe breathes, all living creatures breathe, and the Upanishads tell us that what we seek is "nearer to us than breathing." For a while you come closer to your true nature—that's the inbreath of attention to the Self. Then you are called toward your outer life and you are once more breathing out.

Suffer (in the sense of allow) this movement toward and away from your Self. At the same time, set up reminders that awaken you to a more balanced level of feeling, thinking, and doing. Turn to the wisdom teachers for help. *Keep your thought on your energy in movement*, orders the Tai Chi master. *When you sit, sit; when you cook, cook*, exhorts the Zen roshi.

Remember yourself always and everywhere, cries Gurdjieff. Repeat often his prayer, *I—Wish—To Be*, as you invite the I-consciousness of the wisdom mind to be your guide; affirm the wish to serve in your unfettered heart; and cultivate the vitality of your Body Being so that it has the strength to carry you forward.

Jeanne de Salzmann reminds us that "Our aim is to be able to hold ourselves consciously one day between our two natures. The relationship that we establish there will form our true individuality." Gurdjieff has called this needful place "the third world of man." It is the bridge between our two natures, between, yang and yin, masculine and feminine, action and release.

Each time we are able to bring body, heart, and mind to the same wavelength, we are changed. Yet the mystery of who we are continues to confound us at three in the morning, when body, soul and spirit may seem worlds away from what we think, feel or sense at three in the afternoon.

Forced to suffer this human division, we wonder what Gurdjieff means when he affirms that "the real consciousness is in the subconscious." Or Jung when he invites our conscious ego to explore the unconscious forces within us in search of our true Self. Or Jesus, when he says in the *Gospel of Thomas* that "He who seeks, let him not cease seeking until he finds; and when he finds he will be troubled, and when he is troubled he will be amazed, and he will reign over the All."

We find ourselves *troubled* because after all has been thought and desired and experimented, we are still face to face with the unknown. After a lifetime dedicated to this Work in Life— attempting to be engaged, single-minded, united in purpose rather than pulled in many directions—our question remains: How to stay open to that ongoing call from another level as we go about our daily achieving maneuvers?

If you can acknowledge frankly that you are divided, and that a permanent unification of the multifaceted human being that you are may never take place here on earth, you may be able to stand for a moment between your two natures. Once you have begun to find your way to that elusive space, you will be privileged to live from time to time at the crossroads between yesterday and tomorrow, between earth and heaven.

"Wherever you are is called Here,
And you must treat it as a powerful stranger,
Must ask permission to know it and be known."
David Wagoner

About the Author

Patty de Llosa has studied many spiritual teachings while making her living as a mainstream journalist at *Time, Leisure* and *Fortune* magazines and raising a family in New York and Peru. She began to learn the Gurdjieff sacred dances and movements as a child from Gurdjieff himself in 1948, and has studied and taught them ever since. In 1962 she learned Tai Chi from Master T. T. Liang, just arrived from Formosa, and has continued to practice and teach the long form. Much later she took the three-year training to become an Alexander Technique teacher. And in the last few years has worked with Qigong masters Yang Yang and Robert Peng.

Patty has led group classes, daylong workshops and weeklong intensives in the Gurdjieff work, Tai Chi, Qigong, Taoist meditation, and the Alexander Technique. Among recent public venues are the New York Open Center, Columbia University Graduate Theater Program, Wainwright House and the Lake Conference Center in New York State; Northern Pines Health Resort in Maine; the Peruvian Aikido Association in Lima, Peru; and the Society for Experimental Studies, Toronto.

After graduating from Swarthmore College and the Sorbonne, Patty worked as a reporter for *Time Magazine* for six years in the Business and Art sections. She then married a Peruvian and raised three children in Lima where she also wrote from time to time for the local magazine *Caretas*.

When her husband became governor of Loreto (a jungle province that occupies one-third of Peru), she served as president of The Green Cross, supplying treatment and medicines to the needy in the Amazon jungle, and coordinating with the Peace Corps a summer visit of American doctors to practice there, as well as young people to help build roads and schools. Returning to Lima after a military coup, she founded and ran the first foreign chapter of the

United Nations' pre-school, International Playgroup, for eight years.

On her return to New York, she spent six years as managing editor of *American Fabrics & Fashions Magazine*, moving on to become associate editor of Time Inc. startup magazine *Leisure,* and finally deputy chief of reporters of *Fortune*. She retired in 1999 to take the three-year teacher-training program at the American Center for the Alexander Technique, while working halftime as communications director of internet startup *e-academy, inc*. and writing her first book.

Her previous books are **The Practice of Presence: Five Paths for Daily Life** (Morning Light Press, 2005), **Taming Your Inner Tyrant: A path to healing through dialogues with oneself** (A Spiritual Evolution Press, 2011), and **Finding Time for Your Self: A Spiritual Survivor's Workbook** (Sussex Academic Press, 2015). She also co-edited **Walking the Tightrope: The Jung–Nietzsche Seminars as Taught by Marion Woodman**. Currently, Patty is consulting editor of *Parabola* magazine and *the Daily Good*. She is also a life coach, and teaches Tai Chi, Qigong and the Alexander Technique in New York City.

You can email her at *pattydellosa.com*, where she blogs regularly.

Printed and bound by CPI Group (UK) Ltd, Croydon, CR0 4YY

05/12/2023

08201883-0002